TALMUD
FOR EVERYDAY LIVING

INSIGHTS INTO BUYING AND SELLING

HILLEL GAMORAN

UAHC Press
New York, NY

To Judith, my light, my love.

Acknowledgements

My thanks to the members of Beth Tikvah Congregation in Hoffman Estates, Illinois and Temple Beth Am in Seattle, Washington who studied with me the sections of the Talmud included in this book. Their questions and active participation in class discussions helped me to bring this text into being.

I am deeply indebted to my editor, Rabbi Hara Person. Her careful reading and thoughtful comments have helped to improve each page of this work. I know that she was helped by many people to whom thanks are due, including Debra Hirsch Corman, Jeremy Master, Liane Broido, and Rabbi David Stein. I would also like to thank everyone at the UAHC Press for all their work on behalf of this book, including Ken Gesser, Stuart Benick, and Rick Abrams.

Library of Congress Cataloging-in-Publication Data

Gamoran, Hillel, 1929–
    Talmud for everyday living : insights into buying and selling / Hillel Gamoran.
        p. cm.
    ISBN 0-8074-0815-8 (pbk. : alk. paper)
    1. Business—Religious aspects—Judaism. 2. Business ethics. 3. Ethics, Jewish. 4. Talmud. Bava batra—Criticism, interpretation, etc. 5. Talmud. Bava metzia—Criticism, interpretation, etc. I. Title.

HF5388.G36 2002
296.1'20865—dc21

2002029118

Designer: Shaul Akri
Typesetting: El Ot Ltd., Tel Aviv
This book is printed on acid-free paper.
Copyright © 2003 by Hillel Gamoran
Manufactured in the United States of America

10 9 8 7 6 5 4 3 2 1

Contents

Brief Definitions

Mishnah: The code of Jewish law compiled by Rabbi Judah HaNasi about 200 C.E.

Gemara: The discussion of the law in the academies after the completion of the Mishnah.

Talmud: The Mishnah and the Gemara together. The Jerusalem Talmud was completed about 400 C.E. The Babylonian Talmud was completed about 500 C.E. The selections in this book come from the Babylonian Talmud.

baraita: A statement from the time of the Mishnah, not included in the Mishnah. *Baraitot* (plural) are often cited in the Gemara.

Tanna: A rabbinic Sage from the period of the Mishnah, that is, before 200 C.E.

Amora: A rabbinic Sage of the Gemara, that is, one who lived between 200 and 500 C.E.

Guide to English Text Type

The text of the Talmud in this book is printed in **bold type.**

The editor's comments are in regular type.

THE MISHNAH IS PRINTED IN CAPITAL LETTERS.

THE *BARAITOT* ARE PRINTED IN SMALL CAPITAL LETTERS.

The Gemara is printed in lowercase letters.

Talmudic Sages

TANNAIM

Year C.E. (approx.)	Generation	
	1	R. Yochanan b. Zakkai
90		
	2	R. Akiva, R. Tarfon
130		
	3	R. Meir, R. Simeon, R. Judah, R. Yose, R. Simeon b. Gamaliel, R. Yochanan b. Matya, R. Acha, Abba Saul
160		
	4	R. Judah HaNasi
200		
	5	R. Chiyya
220		

AMORAIM

Year C.E. (approx.)	Generation	Palestine	Babylonia
	1	R. Yannai	Rav, Samuel
250			
	2	R. Yochanan, R. Yose b. Chanina	R. Kahana, R. Huna, Ze'iri, R. Chiyya b. Joseph, R. Judah
290			
	3	R. Eleazar, R. Tachlifa, R. Abahu, R. Samuel b. Isaac, R. Samuel b. Nachmani	R. Nachman, Rabbah, R. Chisda
320			
	4		Abaye, Rava, R. Pappa b. Samuel, Rami b. Chama, R. Nachman b. Isaac
350			
	5		R. Pappa, R. Acha b. R. Ika
375			
	6		R. Ashi

Chapter One

The Purchase Agreement

Bava Metzia 44a

מָשַׁךְ הֵימֶנּוּ פֵּירוֹת וְלֹא נָתַן לוֹ מָעוֹת — אֵינוֹ יָכוֹל לַחֲזוֹר
בּוֹ, נָתַן לוֹ מָעוֹת וְלֹא מָשַׁךְ הֵימֶנּוּ פֵּירוֹת — יָכוֹל לַחֲזוֹר בּוֹ.

The Mishnah deals with the question "When does a sale become
final?" Or to put it in other words, "When is a buyer or a seller no
longer allowed to retract from a purchase agreement?" Does a sale
become final when the buyer takes the goods, or does it become
final when the seller receives the money? The Mishnah answers by
stating the following rule: **A PERSON WHO TAKES GOODS FROM
SOMEONE, BUT HAS NOT PAID THE MONEY, MAY NOT
RETRACT. A PERSON WHO HAS PAID THE MONEY, BUT HAS
NOT TAKEN THE GOODS, MAY RETRACT.**

Bava Metzia 47b

וּמִפְּנֵי מָה אָמְרוּ מְשִׁיכָה קוֹנָה?

גְּזֵירָה שֶׁמָּא יֹאמַר לוֹ נִשְׂרְפוּ חִטֶּיךָ בַּעֲלִיָּיה.

סוֹף סוֹף, מַאן דְּשָׁדָא דְּלֵיקָה בָּעֵי שַׁלּוֹמֵי!

אֶלָּא, גְּזֵירָה שֶׁמָּא תִּפּוֹל דְּלֵיקָה בְּאוֹנֶס.

אִי מוֹקְמַתְּ לְהוּ בִּרְשׁוּתֵיהּ מָסַר נַפְשֵׁיהּ, טָרַח וּמַצִּיל,
וְאִי לָא — לָא מָסַר נַפְשֵׁיהּ טָרַח וּמַצִּיל.

The Talmud has been printed
in a standard form since the
advent of the printing press in
the sixteenth century. The first
sheet is reserved for the title
page; the counting begins on
the second sheet, and the
numbering of the sheets is
marked, front and back, as "a"
and "b." Thus *Bava Metzia* 44a
refers to the front side of sheet
44 in the tractate *Bava Metzia*.

The fourth order of the Mishnah
is called *N'zikin,* "Damages."
It deals with civil and criminal
law. The first three tractates of
N'zikin are called *Bava Kama,
Bava Metzia,* and *Bava Batra,*
meaning "The First Gate," "The
Middle Gate," and "The Last
Gate." In ancient times, courts
were established at the gates of
the cities.

1

The Mishnah states that a sale is completed when a buyer takes the goods, not when a seller receives the money. The Gemara seeks to understand the reason for this ruling: **Why did the Sages say that someone acquires only by taking the goods?**

The Gemara responds: **It was an enactment lest the seller say, "Your wheat was burned in the upper story."** The Rabbis feared that if payment of money defined the completion of a sale, the merchandise that was sold would be at risk until it was delivered. An accident might befall the goods, and the seller could simply say, "Sorry, the wheat that you bought from me was destroyed by fire."

But ultimately, whoever caused the fire would have to pay for the loss. There would be no risk to the buyer because the one who started the fire would have to pay for the loss.

Rather, it was an enactment in case of an accidental fire. We are dealing with a case where no one can be held liable for the fire.

In such a case, **having ownership, the seller would take pains to save it; but otherwise, the seller would not take pains to save it.** The Gemara thus concludes that, for the protection of the buyer's merchandise, a sale should not be deemed final until the buyer has actually taken possession of his purchase.

> ## What's Your Opinion?
>
> Do you agree that if the payment of money finalized a sale, then a seller who was paid for his goods might not be so careful about guarding the buyer's goods? In your view, what is more fair and more reasonable, to consider a sale final when the money is paid or to consider it final when the goods are taken?

Bava Metzia 47b–48a

אֲבָל אָמְרוּ מִי שֶׁפָּרַע מִדּוֹר הַמַּבּוּל הוּא עָתִיד לִיפָּרַע מִמִּי שֶׁאֵינוֹ עוֹמֵד בְּדִיבּוּרוֹ.

אִי אָמְרַתְּ בִּשְׁלָמָא מָעוֹת קוֹנוֹת — מִשּׁוּם הָכִי קָאֵי בְּ"אֲבָל", אֶלָּא אִי אָמְרַתְּ מָעוֹת אֵינָן קוֹנוֹת — אַמַּאי קָאֵי בְּ"אֲבָל"?

מִשּׁוּם דְּבָרִים.

וּבִדְבָרִים מִי קָאֵי בְּ"אֲבָל"? וְהָתַנְיָא, רַבִּי שִׁמְעוֹן אוֹמֵר: אַף עַל פִּי שֶׁאָמְרוּ טַלִּית קוֹנָה דִינַר זָהָב, וְאֵין דִּינַר זָהָב קוֹנֶה טַלִּית — מִכָּל מָקוֹם כָּךְ הֲלָכָה, אֲבָל אָמְרוּ: מִי שֶׁפָּרַע מֵאַנְשֵׁי דוֹר הַמַּבּוּל וּמֵאַנְשֵׁי דוֹר הַפַּלְגָה וּמֵאַנְשֵׁי סְדוֹם וַעֲמוֹרָה וּמִמִּצְרִים בַּיָּם, הוּא עָתִיד לִיפָּרַע מִמִּי שֶׁאֵינוֹ עוֹמֵד בְּדִיבּוּרוֹ. וְהַנּוֹשֵׂא וְנוֹתֵן בִּדְבָרִים — לֹא קָנָה, וְהַחוֹזֵר בּוֹ — אֵין רוּחַ חֲכָמִים נוֹחָה הֵימֶנּוּ.

וְאָמַר רָבָא: אָנוּ אֵין לָנוּ אֶלָּא "אֵין רוּחַ חֲכָמִים נוֹחָה הֵימֶנּוּ".

דְּבָרִים וְאִיכָּא בַּהֲדַיְיהוּ מָעוֹת — קָאֵי בְּ"אֲבָל", דְּבָרִים וְלֵיכָּא בַּהֲדַיְיהוּ מָעוֹת — לָא קָאֵי בְּ"אֲבָל".

The Mishnah continues: **BUT THE SAGES SAID: THE ONE WHO PUNISHED THE GENERATION OF THE FLOOD WILL PUNISH THOSE WHO DO NOT STAND BY THEIR WORD.**

If an agreement for a sale has been reached, but the buyer has not yet taken the goods, the Mishnah states that the parties may still retract. In such a case, the court will not penalize someone who retracts from the agreement. Nevertheless, the Sages maintain that God will punish persons who promise to buy or sell and then break their word.

The Gemara raises a question: **If you had said that a sale was finalized by the payment of money, then it could be understood why someone who retracted after the money was paid would be subject to punishment by God, but since you said that a sale is not finalized by the payment of money, why should anyone be subject to punishment for retracting?** Since both buyer and seller are aware that, even though money has been paid, the sale is not final until the goods

Although the talmudic Sages believed in the court system where wrongs could be righted, they also recognized the limitations of any human system of law. They held that, ultimately, the deficiencies of the courts would be corrected by God. In this case under discussion, they maintained that just as God punished the evildoers at the time of the Flood, so would God punish those who broke their word.

are taken, why should someone who backs out before the goods are taken be subject to punishment by God?

The Gemara answers: **Because of words.** Although we are not legally bound to complete the sale, we are morally bound to do so because we gave our word, and if we fail to do so, we are subject to punishment.

What's Your Opinion?

Is it right that someone who agrees to a sale, accepts payment, and promises to deliver the goods is not forced by the court to follow through on the commitment? Is it right that, in such a case, the one who retracts should be punished by God?

Consider This Case

Reuben and Simon agreed on the sale price for twenty barrels of wine. They shook hands, and Reuben paid for the wine, which Simon promised to deliver in two weeks.

In the meantime, there was a sudden rise in the price of wine, and Simon had second thoughts about the deal. He was not a wealthy man and had great need for additional income from the sale of his wine. He decided to cancel the sale and return the money to Reuben. Reuben, however, didn't want the sale to be cancelled. He wanted to receive his wine at the agreed price. In your opinion, what should the court do?

Force Simon to deliver the wine?

Not force Simon to deliver the wine, but invoke God's punishment on him for not keeping his word?

Allow Simon to repay the money and cancel the sale?

Something else?

The Gemara then challenges the notion that one who does not stand by his word is subject to punishment by God: **But is one subject to punishment by God because of words? For surely it has been taught in a *baraita*: RABBI SIMEON SAID: EVEN THOUGH THE RABBIS SAID: BY TAKING A GARMENT, ONE ACQUIRES**

A GOLD *DINAR,* BUT BY TAKING A GOLD *DINAR,* ONE DOES NOT ACQUIRE A GARMENT, AND THIS IS INDEED THE LAW, BUT THEY SAID: **THE ONE WHO PUNISHED THE PEOPLE OF THE GENERATION OF THE FLOOD, AND THE PEOPLE OF THE GENERATION OF THE DISPERSION, AND THE PEOPLE OF SODOM AND GOMORRAH, AND THE EGYPTIANS AT THE SEA, WILL PUNISH THOSE WHO DO NOT STAND BY THEIR WORD.** Up to this point, the *baraita* is similar to the Mishnah. It reiterates the rule that although the payment of money does not complete a sale, a person who breaks his word is subject to punishment by God. The *baraita* then adds: **AND SOMEONE WHO DOES BUSINESS WITH WORDS DOES NOT ACQUIRE, BUT THE SPIRIT OF THE SAGES IS NOT PLEASED WITH SOMEONE WHO BACKS OUT OF A VERBAL COMMITMENT.**

The Gemara comments on the last part of the *baraita:* **And Rava said: We have no other condemnation than "the spirit of the Sages is not pleased."** Rava sees a difference in terms of punishment between the first part and the last part of the *baraita.* In the first, the outcome of not standing by one's word is punishment by God. In the last, it is the displeasure of the Sages. Surely being subject to the Sages' disapproval is not as harsh as being subject to punishment by God.

The Gemara resolves the contradiction: **Words that have money together with them are subject to punishment by God; words that do not have money together with them are not subject to punishment by God.**

The Gemara thus accounts for three different situations when, for example, Levi and Judah strike a deal for the sale of wheat.

1. If Levi, the buyer, takes the wheat and later changes his mind and wants to return it rather than pay for it, the court will enforce the sale and require Levi to pay for the wheat.

2. If Levi pays for the wheat but has not yet picked it up, and later Judah changes his mind and wants to cancel the sale and return the money, the court will not prevent him from doing so. However, Judah, according to the court, will be subject to punishment by God for having broken his word after the money was paid.

The generation of the dispersion refers to the story in Genesis, chapter 11. The people, in their arrogance, planned to build a tower that would reach to the sky, perhaps to challenge God. God punished them by confusing their speech and scattering them over the face of the earth.

Rabbi Simeon bar Yochai, normally called Rabbi Simeon in the Mishnah, was one of the leading students of Rabbi Akiva. His views are often cited as being at odds with those of Rabbi Akiva's other students. Rabbi Simeon spent many years in hiding from the Romans, and an aura of mystery grew up about his life. Numerous stories were told about him as a miracle worker, and until recent times, it was believed that he was the author of the *Zohar,* the major kabbalistic text. His views are recorded in the Mishnah over 300 times.

Rava was the foremost Sage of the Babylonian Talmud. He lived in the middle of the fourth century and founded an academy at Mechoza on the Tigris River. His name appears in the Talmud more often than any other teacher, and his decisions are usually cited as authoritative. His debates with Abaye, as recorded in the Gemara, represent the high point of talmudic reasoning and rhetoric. Many rulings of Rava are cited by the Sages of later generations.

3. If neither money nor merchandise exchanges hands, the court will not enforce an agreement that Levi and Judah have made; neither will the Rabbis invoke God's punishment on either party, but the Sages will be displeased with those who break their word.

What's Your Opinion?

Do you agree with the three ways in which the *Amoraim* dealt with those who reneged on sales agreements? Are they fair? How could they improved?

Consider This Case

Lynne hadn't played her piano in many years and decided to sell it. Martha offered Lynne $1,000 for the piano. Lynne agreed. Martha gave Lynne a check for $1,000 and said that she would look for a company to move the piano.

The next evening, Robert was at Lynne's house. Lynne told Robert about the sale of her piano. Robert said that it was ridiculous to sell that piano for $1,000. He said that he would give her $2,000 for it. Lynne really needed the additional $1,000 and thought that she would return Martha's check to her and accept Robert's offer, but she wasn't sure if that was the right thing to do.

What should Lynne do? What would you do if you were Lynne?

Bava Metzia 48b

"אֲבָל אָמְרוּ מִי שֶׁפָּרַע וכו׳".

אִיתְּמַר, אַבַּיֵי אָמַר: אוֹדוּעֵי מוֹדְעִינַן לֵיה, רָבָא אָמַר: מֵילָט לָיְיטִינַן לֵיה.

אַבַּיֵי אָמַר: אוֹדוּעֵי מוֹדְעִינַן לֵיה, דִּכְתִיב "וְנָשִׂיא בְעַמְּךָ לֹא תָאֹר".

רָבָא אָמַר: מֵילָט לָיְיטִינַן לֵיה, דִּכְתִיב "בְעַמְּךָ" — בְּעוֹשֶׂה מַעֲשֵׂה עַמְּךָ. — אָמַר רָבָא: מְנָא אָמִינָא לָה — דְּרַבִּי חִיָּיא

בַּר יוֹסֵף יָהֲבוּ לֵיהּ זוּזֵי אַמַּלְחָא, לְסוֹף אַיְיקַר מִלְחָא. אֲתָא לְקַמֵּיהּ דְּרַבִּי יוֹחָנָן, אֲמַר לֵיהּ: זִיל הַב לְהוּ, וְאִי לָא — קַבֵּיל עֲלָךְ מִי שֶׁפָּרַע.

וְאִי אָמְרַתְּ אוֹדוּעֵי מוֹדְעִינַן לֵיהּ, רַבִּי חִיָּיא בַּר יוֹסֵף בַּר אוֹדוּעֵי הוּא?

וְאֶלָּא מַאי? מֵילָט לָיְיטִינַן לֵיהּ? רַבִּי חִיָּיא בַּר יוֹסֵף אָתֵי לְקַבּוּלֵי עֲלֵיהּ לְטוּתָא דְּרַבָּנָן?

אֶלָּא רַבִּי חִיָּיא בַּר יוֹסֵף עֵרָבוֹן הוּא דְּיָהֲבֵי לֵיהּ. הוּא סָבַר: כְּנֶגְדּוֹ הוּא קוֹנֶה, וַאֲמַר לֵיהּ רַבִּי יוֹחָנָן: כְּנֶגֶד כּוּלּוֹ הוּא קוֹנֶה.

The Mishnah had stated: **BUT THE SAGES SAID, "THE ONE WHO PUNISHED THE GENERATION OF THE FLOOD WILL PUNISH THOSE WHO DO NOT STAND BY THEIR WORD."**

The Gemara now continues speaking of a person who backed out of a sale after money had been paid: **It was stated: Abaye said: We make it known that one who backs out of a verbal commitment will be punished by God. Rava said: We actually invoke a curse,** thus seeking, in fact, to bring God's punishment on those who break their word.

Abaye said: We make it known that God's punishment will be forthcoming, **for it is written in the Torah, "You shall not curse a prince among your people"** (Exod. 22:27). In this regard, Abaye, considering all the people as princes, did not want to take the harsh step of actually cursing the wrongdoer and perhaps bringing down a terrible divine punishment.

Rava said: We invoke a curse, for it is written, "among your people," referring to one who acts according to the way the people should act. According to Rava, a person who breaks a promise is excluded from the protection against curses that the biblical verse provides and thus should indeed be cursed by the Sages.

Abaye was a leading Sage of the fourth century who served, near the end of his life, as the head of the academy at Pumbedita. He earned his livelihood as a farmer and a wine trader. He is best known for the numerous debates recorded in the Talmud in which he and his colleague Rava engaged. They demonstrate his vast knowledge of the received traditions and his sharp, probing mind. Although, in most cases, the Gemara preferred the views of Rava over his, Abaye's arguments and reasoning had a lasting influence on Jewish law.

What's Your Opinion?

Whose view do you favor, Abaye's or Rava's? Should the court ever curse individuals who have acted within the letter of the law, but have broken their word? Is there another way that they should be punished or reproved?

Rabbi Yochanan bar Nappacha (blacksmith) is referred to in the Talmud simply as Rabbi Yochanan. He lived in Palestine during the third century and served for many years as the head of the academy in Tiberias. He was the leading Sage of his time, and his teachings are among the most important in the talmudic literature. He is mentioned more often than any other authority in the Jerusalem Talmud, and he had wide influence on rulings in the Babylonian Talmud as well. Some have credited Rabbi Yochanan with being the editor of the Jerusalem Talmud; although this cannot be so, as it was not completed until more than a century after his death, his imprint on it can be seen on most of its pages.

Rabbi Chiyya bar Joseph, a third-century Babylonian *Amora,* was a student of Rav and Samuel. He emigrated to Palestine, where he became a student of Rabbi Yochanan. It is evident from our text that he was a merchant.

Rava then defends his position by citing an actual decision in a court case. **Rava said: How do I know that my view is correct? Some people gave money to Rabbi Chiyya bar Joseph for salt. Later, salt went up in price,** and Rabbi Chiyya wanted to cancel the sale and return the money. **He came before Rabbi Yochanan. Rabbi Yochanan said to him: Go and give them the salt, for if not, you must accept God's punishment upon yourself.**

The Gemara now points out that in view of the court case just cited, Abaye's opinion is untenable. **And if you should say that we merely inform him that he will be subject to God's punishment for not standing by his word, did Rabbi Chiyya bar Joseph need to be informed?** Surely, as a rabbinic scholar, he was aware of the consequences of breaking a promise and didn't need to be informed of the law.

Although Abaye's position is undermined, the Gemara shows that Rava's view is also incompatible with the court case. **What then should be done? Should we curse him? Would Rabbi Chiyya bar Joseph come to accept a curse of the Rabbis upon himself?** Is it reasonable to imagine that Rabbi Chiyya would have come to court to be cursed?

What happened in Rabbi Yochanan's court cannot be explained either in accordance with Abaye's view or in accordance with Rava's view. The Gemara then suggests that the circumstances of the case are different than we had been led to believe. **Rather, it was a deposit that they gave to Rabbi Chiyya bar Joseph.** An agreement was made to purchase a certain amount of salt, and the buyers gave Rabbi Chiyya bar Joseph a down payment toward the purchase. **He believed that they had acquired salt equal in value to the deposit** and that he did not have to sell them the rest of the salt they had ordered, **but Rabbi Yochanan told him that, with the deposit, they had acquired the entire purchase** and that he was subject to God's punishment if he did not give them all of the salt that he had promised to sell them.

Bava Metzia 49a

רַב כָּהֲנָא יָהֲבִי לֵיהּ זוּזֵי אַכִּיתָנָא, לַסּוֹף אַייַקַּר כִּיתָנָא. אֲתָא לְקַמֵּיהּ דְּרַב. אֲמַר לֵיהּ: בְּמַאי דִּנְקִיטַת זוּזֵי — הַב לְהוּ, וְאִידָךְ — דְּבָרִים נִינְהוּ, וּדְבָרִים אֵין בָּהֶן מִשּׁוּם מְחוּסְרֵי אֲמָנָה.

דְּאִיתְּמַר: דְּבָרִים, רַב אָמַר: אֵין בָּהֶן מִשּׁוּם מְחוּסְרֵי אֲמָנָה, וְרַבִּי יוֹחָנָן אָמַר: יֵשׁ בָּהֶם מִשּׁוּם מְחוּסְרֵי אֲמָנָה.

Rav's view on this matter is illustrated in the following case: **Some people gave money to Rav Kahana as a deposit for flax. Later the flax went up in price. Rav Kahana came before Rav. Rav said to him, "For that part against which you are holding money, give them flax, but the rest are words, and words do not involve a breach of trust."** Rav thus ruled in court that Rav Kahana was under no legal obligation to complete the sale, for no goods had been taken, and he was under no moral obligation to deliver flax except for that portion of the flax that was covered by the deposit. The rest was mere words, and all concerned knew that words do not create a binding contract.

Rav's ruling in the case of Rav Kahana's sale of flax is the opposite of Rabbi Yochanan's ruling in the case of Rabbi Chiyya selling salt. Rav believes that even though a buyer promises to buy a large quantity of product, only the merchandise equal in value to the deposit is acquired; the rest are mere words. But Rabbi Yochanan holds that because of the promise, the buyer acquires the entire purchase: **It was stated regarding words, Rav says: When a promise is made, but the money is not paid for the goods, it does not involve a breach of trust. But Rav Yochanan says: It does involve a breach of trust.**

There were a number of Sages named Rav Kahana. The Sage mentioned here is clearly the early third-century disciple of Rav. At some point Rav Kahana left Babylonia and was associated with the great second-generation *Amoraim* of Palestine, Rabbi Yochanan and Resh Lakish; later he returned to Babylonia.

9

With whom do you agree, Rabbi Yochanan or Rav? Is a person under a moral obligation to follow through on a promise even if the other party knows that words do not create a binding agreement? Suppose the price of flax doubles or triples, and suppose Rav Kahana would have to buy the flax at the new price in order to have enough flax to fulfill his promise, is he still morally obligated to complete the entire sale, as Rabbi Yochanan believes, or would giving flax equal to the deposit, as Rav holds, be sufficient?

Consider This Case

Martin was the Owner of Sunshine Orange Farm in California's Central Valley. He often made arrangements to sell his fruit before it was picked. In the winter of 1998–99, Albert, a wholesaler, who bought produce from farmers and sold it to supermarkets, contracted to buy 2,000 standard boxes ($37\frac{1}{2}$ pounds each) of oranges from Martin at a price of $10 per box. He paid Martin $2,000, which was 10 percent of the total cost, and agreed to pay the balance when the oranges were delivered.

Soon after their agreement was made, the Central Valley suffered a rare and devastating freeze. Temperatures reached a fruit-killing twenty-one degrees. The governor declared a state of emergency in four counties. Much of California's orange crop was destroyed. Martin lost 90 percent of his crop. The wholesale price of oranges climbed to $25 per box.

Martin was aware that he would not make any profit this winter, but he hoped to make the best of a bad situation. He was willing to deliver to Albert the 200 boxes of oranges for which Albert had already paid, but he felt that he simply could not afford to deliver the balance of the oranges to Albert at $10 a box, since the other 1,800 boxes were now worth $25 each on the open market. He offered to deliver the 1,800 boxes to Albert at $20. But Albert insisted on the completion of the sale at the terms to which they had both freely agreed, $10 per box. "A signed contract," he said, "is binding, and Martin should stick by his word."

What do you think Martin should do? Who is right?

מֵיתִיבִי, רַבִּי שִׁמְעוֹן אוֹמֵר: אַף עַל פִּי שֶׁאָמְרוּ טַלִּית קוֹנָה
דִּינַר זָהָב וְאֵין דִּינַר זָהָב קוֹנֶה טַלִּית, מִכָּל מָקוֹם כָּךְ הֲלָכָה,
אֲבָל אָמְרוּ: מִי שֶׁפָּרַע מֵאַנְשֵׁי דּוֹר הַמַּבּוּל וּמֵאַנְשֵׁי דּוֹר
הַפְלָגָה — הוּא עָתִיד לִיפָּרַע מִמִּי שֶׁאֵינוֹ עוֹמֵד בְּדִיבּוּרוֹ!

תַּנָּאֵי הִיא, דִּתְנַן: מַעֲשֶׂה בְּרַבִּי יוֹחָנָן בֶּן מַתְיָא שֶׁאָמַר לִבְנוֹ:
צֵא וּשְׂכוֹר לָנוּ פוֹעֲלִים. הָלַךְ וּפָסַק לָהֶם מְזוֹנוֹת. וּכְשֶׁבָּא
אֵצֶל אָבִיו אָמַר לוֹ: בְּנִי, אֲפִילוּ אַתָּה עוֹשֶׂה לָהֶם כִּסְעוּדַת
שְׁלֹמֹה בְּשַׁעְתּוֹ לֹא יָצָאתָ יְדֵי חוֹבָתְךָ עִמָּהֶם, שֶׁהֵן בְּנֵי
אַבְרָהָם יִצְחָק וְיַעֲקֹב. אֶלָּא, עַד שֶׁלֹּא יַתְחִילוּ בִּמְלָאכָה צֵא
וֶאֱמוֹר לָהֶם: עַל מְנָת שֶׁאֵין לָכֶם עָלַי אֶלָּא פַּת וְקִטְנִית
בִּלְבָד.

וְאִי סָלְקָא דַּעְתָּךְ דְּבָרִים יֵשׁ בָּהֶן מִשּׁוּם מְחוּסְּרֵי אֲמָנָה —
הֵיכִי אָמַר לֵיהּ זִיל הֲדַר בָּךְ?

שָׁאנֵי הָתָם, דְּפוֹעֲלִים גּוּפַיְיהוּ לָא סָמְכָא דַּעְתַּיְיהוּ. מַאי
טַעְמָא — מֵידַע יָדְעִי דְּעַל אֲבוּהּ סָמַךְ.

The Gemara now cites a *baraita,* which appears to contradict Rav:
**They raised an objection. "RABBI SIMEON SAYS: EVEN THOUGH
THEY SAID: BY TAKING A GARMENT, ONE ACQUIRES A GOLD *DINAR,* BUT
BY TAKING A GOLD *DINAR,* ONE DOES NOT ACQUIRE A GARMENT, AND
THIS IS INDEED THE LAW, BUT THEY SAID: THE ONE WHO PUNISHED THE
PEOPLE OF THE GENERATION OF THE FLOOD, AND THE PEOPLE OF THE
GENERATION OF THE DISPERSION, WILL PUNISH THOSE WHO DO NOT
STAND BY THEIR WORD."** The words of Rabbi Simeon in the *baraita*
are unambiguous. They clearly support the position of Rabbi
Yochanan that verbal commitments are moral obligations. Since
Rabbi Simeon is a *Tanna,* and an *Amora* (Rav) cannot contradict a
Tanna, it would appear that Rav's position has been overruled.

The Gemara then suggests that there may be another *Tanna* who
disputes Rabbi Simeon: **It is a dispute between *Tannaim,* for
we have learned in a *baraita:* IT ONCE HAPPENED THAT RABBI
YOCHANAN BEN MATYA SAID TO HIS SON, "GO OUT AND HIRE WORKERS
FOR US." HE WENT AND PROMISED THEM FOOD. BUT WHEN HE CAME TO
HIS FATHER, HE SAID TO HIM, "MY SON, EVEN IF YOU MAKE A MEAL FOR**

Rabbi Yochanan ben Matya is
mentioned in the Talmud only
here. He was a *Tanna* who
lived in the second century.

11

THEM LIKE SOLOMON'S FEAST IN HIS TIME, YOU HAVE NOT FULFILLED YOUR OBLIGATION TOWARD THEM, FOR THEY ARE CHILDREN OF ABRAHAM, ISAAC, AND JACOB. RATHER, BEFORE THEY BEGIN WORK, GO OUT AND SAY TO THEM, 'YOU ARE HIRED ON CONDITION THAT YOU HAVE NO CLAIM WITH ME EXCEPT FOR JUST BREAD AND BEANS.'"

The Gemara cites this *baraita* to show that Rabbi Yochanan ben Matya, a rabbinic scholar, went ahead and changed a verbal agreement. **For if you should be of the opinion that words involve a breach of trust, how could he say to him, "Go, retract"?** Rabbi Yochanan ben Matya must have believed that one could change a verbal agreement without breaking any moral code. Thus he appears to dispute the view of Rabbi Simeon and to support the position of Rav that a buyer can cancel an oral agreement.

But the Gemara sees a flaw in drawing such a conclusion from the case of Rabbi Yochanan ben Matya: **It is different there, for the workers themselves did not rely on the son's words. What is the reason? They know that he is dependent on his father.** Since this is a case where the workers did not rely on the son's promise in the first place, we cannot conclude that Rabbi Yochanan ben Matya is of the opinion that, in general, a person is allowed to renege on his promises.

Thus the statement of Rabbi Simeon in the *baraita,* that "the Sages are not pleased with someone who backs out of a verbal commitment," stands as authoritative. Rav's position is rejected, and that of Rabbi Yochanan is sustained.

R E V I E W I N G   T H E   T E X T

Bava Metzia 44a

Mishnah: **IF A PERSON TAKES GOODS FROM SOMEONE, BUT HAS NOT PAID THE MONEY, HE MAY NOT RETRACT. IF A PERSON HAS PAID MONEY, BUT HAS NOT TAKEN THE GOODS, HE MAY RETRACT.**

Bava Metzia 47b

Gemara: **Why did the Sages say that someone acquires only by taking the goods?**

It was an enactment lest the seller say, "Your wheat was burned in the upper story."

But ultimately, whoever caused the fire would have to pay for the loss.

Rather, it was an enactment in case of an accidental fire.

Having ownership, the seller would take pains to save it; but otherwise, the seller would not take pains to save it.

Bava Metzia 47b–48a

Mishnah: **BUT THE SAGES SAID: THE ONE WHO PUNISHED THE GENERATION OF THE FLOOD WILL PUNISH THOSE WHO DO NOT STAND BY THEIR WORD.**

Gemara: **If the you had said that a sale was finalized by the payment of money, then it could be understood why someone who retracted after the money was paid would be subject to punishment by God, but since you said that a sale is not finalized by the payment of money, why should anyone be subject to punishment for retracting?**

Because of words.

But is one subject to punishment by God because of words? For surely it has been taught in a *baraita*: RABBI SIMEON SAID: EVEN THOUGH THE RABBIS SAID: BY TAKING A GARMENT, ONE ACQUIRES A GOLD *DINAR*, BUT BY TAKING A GOLD *DINAR*, ONE DOES NOT ACQUIRE A GARMENT, AND THIS IS INDEED THE LAW, BUT THEY SAID: THE ONE WHO PUNISHED THE PEOPLE OF THE GENERATION OF THE FLOOD, AND THE PEOPLE OF THE GENERATION OF THE DISPERSION, AND THE PEOPLE OF SODOM AND GOMORRAH, AND THE EGYPTIANS AT THE SEA, WILL PUNISH THOSE WHO DO NOT STAND BY THEIR WORD. AND SOMEONE WHO DOES BUSINESS WITH WORDS DOES NOT ACQUIRE, BUT THE SPIRIT OF THE SAGES IS NOT PLEASED WITH SOMEONE WHO BACKS OUT OF A VERBAL COMMITMENT.

And Rava said: We have no other condemnation than "the spirit of the Sages is not pleased."

Words that have money together with them are subject to punishment by God; words that do not have money together with them are not subject to punishment by God.

Mishnah: **BUT THE SAGES SAID, "THE ONE WHO PUNISHED THE GENERATION OF THE FLOOD WILL PUNISH THOSE WHO DO NOT STAND BY THEIR WORD."**

Gemara: **It was stated: Abaye said: We make it known that one who backs out of a verbal commitment will be punished by God. Rava said: We actually invoke a curse.**

Abaye said: We make it known, for it is written in the Torah, "You shall not curse a prince among your people."

Rava said: We invoke a curse, for it is written, "among your people," referring to one who acts according to the way the people should act.

Rava said: How do I know that my view is correct? Some people gave money to Rabbi Chiyya bar Joseph for salt. Later, salt went up in price. He came before Rabbi Yochanan. Rabbi Yochanan said to him: Go and give them the salt, for if not, you must accept God's punishment upon yourself.

And if you should say that we merely inform him that he will be subject to God's punishment for not standing by his word, did Rabbi Chiyya bar Joseph need to be informed?

What then should be done? Should we curse him? Would Rabbi Chiyya bar Joseph come to accept a curse of the Rabbis upon himself?

Rather, it was a deposit that they gave to Rabbi Chiyya bar Joseph. He believed that they had acquired salt equal in value to the deposit, but Rabbi Yochanan told him that, with the deposit, they had acquired the entire purchase.

Some people gave money to Rav Kahana as a deposit for flax. Later the flax went up in price. Rav Kahana came before Rav. Rav said to him, "For that part against which you are holding money, give them flax, but the rest are words and words do not involve a breach of trust."

It was stated regarding words, Rav says: When a promise is made, but the money is not paid for the goods, it does not involve a breach of trust. But Rav Yochanan says: It does involve a breach of trust.

Bava Metzia 49a

They raised an objection. "RABBI SIMEON SAYS: EVEN THOUGH THEY SAID: BY TAKING A GARMENT ONE ACQUIRES A GOLD *DINAR*, BUT BY TAKING A GOLD *DINAR*, ONE DOES NOT ACQUIRE A GARMENT, AND THIS IS INDEED THE LAW, BUT THEY SAID: THE ONE WHO PUNISHED THE PEOPLE OF THE GENERATION OF THE FLOOD, AND THE PEOPLE OF THE GENERATION OF THE DISPERSION, WILL PUNISH THOSE WHO DO NOT STAND BY THEIR WORD."

It is a dispute between *Tannaim,* for we have learned in a *baraita:* IT ONCE HAPPENED THAT RABBI YOCHANAN BEN MATYA SAID TO HIS SON, "GO OUT AND HIRE WORKERS FOR US." HE WENT AND PROMISED THEM FOOD. BUT WHEN HE CAME TO HIS FATHER, HE SAID TO HIM, "MY SON, EVEN IF YOU MAKE A MEAL FOR THEM LIKE SOLOMON'S FEAST IN HIS TIME, YOU HAVE NOT FULFILLED YOUR OBLIGATION TOWARD THEM, FOR THEY ARE CHILDREN OF ABRAHAM, ISAAC, AND JACOB. RATHER, BEFORE THEY BEGIN WORK, GO OUT AND SAY TO THEM, 'YOU ARE HIRED ON CONDITION THAT YOU HAVE NO CLAIM WITH ME EXCEPT FOR JUST BREAD AND BEANS.'"

For if you should be of the opinion that words involve a breach of trust, how could he say to him, "Go, retract"?

It is different there, for the workers themselves did not rely on the son's words. What is the reason? They know that he is dependent on his father.

Chapter Two

What Is Included in a Sale?

מָכַר אֶת הַקָרוֹן — לֹא מָכַר אֶת הַפְּרָדוֹת, מָכַר אֶת הַפְּרָדוֹת — לֹא מָכַר אֶת הַקָרוֹן.

מָכַר אֶת הַצֶּמֶד — לֹא מָכַר אֶת הַבָּקָר, מָכַר אֶת הַבָּקָר — לֹא מָכַר אֶת הַצֶּמֶד.

רַבִּי יְהוּדָה אוֹמֵר: הַדָּמִים מוֹדִיעִין; כֵּיצַד? אָמַר לוֹ: "מְכוֹר לִי צִימְדָּךְ בְּמָאתַיִם זוּז", הַדָּבָר יָדוּעַ שֶׁאֵין הַצֶּמֶד בְּמָאתַיִם זוּז. וַחֲכָמִים אוֹמְרִים: אֵין הַדָּמִים רְאָיָה.

תָּנֵי רַב תַּחְלִיפָא בַּר מַעַרְבָא קַמֵּיה דְּרַבִּי אַבָּהוּ: מָכַר אֶת הַקָרוֹן — מָכַר אֶת הַפְּרָדוֹת.

וְהָא אֲנַן "לֹא מָכַר" תְּנַן!

אָמַר לֵיה: אִיסְמְיֵיה?

אָמַר לֵיה: לָא, תִּיתַרְגֵּם מַתְנִיתֶךְ בַּאֲדוּקִין בּוֹ.

"מָכַר אֶת הַצֶּמֶד — לֹא מָכַר אֶת הַבָּקָר" וכו'.

הֵיכִי דָּמֵי? אִילֵימָא דְּקָרוּ לְצִימְדָּא צִימְדָּא, וּלְבָקָר בָּקָר — פְּשִׁיטָא, צִימְדָּא זַבִּין לֵיה, בָּקָר לָא זַבִּין לֵיה! וְאֶלָּא דְּקָרוּ לֵיה נַמִי לְבָקָר צִימְדָּא — כּוּלֵיה זַבִּין לֵיה!

לָא צְרִיכָא, בְּאַתְרָא דְּקָרוּ לֵיהּ לְצִימְדָא צִימְדָא, וְלִבְקַר —
בְּקַר, וְאִיכָּא נַמִי דְּקָרוּ לִבְקַר צִימְדָא; רַבִּי יְהוּדָה סָבַר:
הַדָּמִים מוֹדִיעִין, וְרַבָּנַן סָבְרִי: אֵין הַדָּמִים רְאָיָה.

Mishnah: **IF SOMEONE SOLD A WAGON, IT CANNOT BE ASSUMED THAT THE MULES WERE SOLD ALONG WITH IT. IF SOMEONE SOLD SOME MULES, IT CANNOT BE ASSUMED THAT THE WAGON WAS SOLD ALONG WITH THEM.**

IF SOMEONE SOLD A YOKE, IT CANNOT BE ASSUMED THAT THE OXEN WERE SOLD ALONG WITH IT. IF SOMEONE SOLD SOME OXEN, IT CANNOT BE ASSUMED THAT THE YOKE WAS SOLD ALONG WITH THEM.

RABBI JUDAH SAYS: THE PURCHASE PRICE CAN INDICATE WHAT WAS SOLD. HOW SO? IF ONE SAID TO THE OTHER: SELL ME YOUR YOKE FOR 200 ZUZ, IT IS OBVIOUS THAT THE YOKE ALONE DOES NOT COST 200 ZUZ. BUT THE SAGES SAY: THE PRICE IS NO PROOF.

A *baraita* is cited in the Gemara, which contradicts our Mishnah: **Rav Tachlifa the Westerner taught the following *baraita* before Rabbi Abahu:** IF SOMEONE SOLD A WAGON, IT CAN BE ASSUMED THAT THE MULES WERE SOLD ALONG WITH IT.

Rabbi Abahu replied: But we learned in the Mishnah that we *cannot* assume that the mules were sold along with it.

So Rav Tachlifa asked of him: Shall I delete the *baraita*? The *baraitot* were introduced into the academy's discussions from memory. In this case, the teaching of the *baraita* is exactly the opposite as that of the Mishnah. Rav Tachlifa may have feared that he had misheard the *baraita* or that the *baraita* was in error and therefore should be deleted.

Rabbi Abahu answered him: No, explain your *baraita* as referring to a case where the mules are attached to the wagon. A buyer who saw the mules attached to the wagon, might have reason to believe that they were included in the sale.

The Mishnah said: **IF SOMEONE SOLD A YOKE, IT CANNOT BE ASSUMED THAT THE OXEN WERE SOLD ALONG WITH IT. IF SOMEONE SOLD SOME OXEN, IT CANNOT BE ASSUMED THAT**

When the Mishnah speaks of Rabbi Judah, without his father's name, it refers to Rabbi Judah bar Ilai, who lived during the middle of the second century. He was a student of Rabbi Akiva and was among those who had to be ordained secretly because of persecution by Roman authorities. When the persecution died down, Rabbi Judah took the lead in reconvening the Sanhedrin, the supreme rabbinic court. He was one of the most learned and respected Rabbis of his time and was recognized as the chief spokesman among the Sages. His opinions are recorded in the Mishnah over 600 times.

A *zuz* was a silver coin frequently used in business dealings in talmudic times. The well-known Aramaic Passover song "Chad Gadya" speaks of a father who bought a kid for two *zuzim*, the plural of *zuz*.

Rabbi Abahu was a third/fourth-century Palestinian *Amora*. He was the principal student of Rabbi Yochanan and became the head of the academy in Caesarea. He knew the Greek language well and represented the Jewish people to the Romans.

Rav Tachlifa was a Palestinian *Amora* who lived in the early part of the fourth century. He spent a period of time in Babylonia, and because his origin was Palestine, he became known as "the Westerner." Rav Tachlifa was a student of Rabbi Abahu.

THAT THE YOKE WAS SOLD ALONG WITH THEM. RABBI JUDAH SAYS: THE PURCHASE PRICE CAN INDICATE WHAT WAS SOLD.

The Gemara considers the circumstances under which Rabbi Judah and the Sages disagree: **What are the circumstances of the case? If the purchase was made in a place where the term "yoke" referred to a yoke alone and the term "oxen" referred to oxen alone, then it is obvious that the yoke was sold and not the oxen,** and Rabbi Judah would not question the ruling. **But if the purchase was made in a place where oxen were also included in the term "yoke,"** where oxen were normally sold along with the yoke, **then the seller could indeed have sold everything,** and even the Rabbis would agree that a high price would be an indication that the oxen were included.

No, it was necessary to state the dispute between Rabbi Judah and the Sages to account for a place where some people used the term "yoke" to refer to a yoke alone and the term "oxen" to refer to oxen alone, while others included oxen in the term "yoke." In such a case, Rabbi Judah was of the opinion that the price could indicate whether oxen were included in the sale, whereas the Sages maintained that the price was no proof.

What's Your Opinion?

Do you believe that there are situations when the price can help determine what is included in a sale? Give some examples of such situations.

Over the phone, Jesse was given a price quote for a certain computer by A&B Computers. It is a forty-five-minute drive from Jesse's house to the A&B store, but he didn't mind the drive because the price was a huge bargain for this particular computer. When he got to the store, Jesse was told that the price quoted to him over the phone did not include a monitor. Jesse was furious. He said that a computer without a monitor was useless and that A&B should include a monitor for the same price. The A&B salesman said that Jesse should have realized that at that price there was no way a monitor would have been included.

Who do you think is right in the dispute between Jesse and the computer store?

REVIEWING THE TEXT

Bava Batra 77b

Mishnah: **IF SOMEONE SOLD A WAGON, IT CANNOT BE ASSUMED THAT THE MULES WERE SOLD ALONG WITH IT. IF SOMEONE SOLD SOME MULES, IT CANNOT BE ASSUMED THAT THE WAGON WAS SOLD ALONG WITH THEM.**

IF SOMEONE SOLD A YOKE, IT CANNOT BE ASSUMED THAT THE OXEN WERE SOLD ALONG WITH IT. IF SOMEONE SOLD SOME OXEN, IT CANNOT BE ASSUMED THAT THE YOKE WAS SOLD ALONG WITH THEM.

RABBI JUDAH SAYS: THE PURCHASE PRICE CAN INDICATE WHAT WAS SOLD. HOW SO? IF ONE SAID TO ANOTHER: SELL ME YOUR YOKE FOR 200 *ZUZ*, IT IS OBVIOUS THAT THE YOKE ALONE DOES NOT COST 200 *ZUZ*. BUT THE SAGES SAY: THE PRICE IS NO PROOF.

Gemara: **Rav Tachlifa the Westerner taught the following *baraita* before Rabbi Abahu: IF SOMEONE SOLD A WAGON, IT CAN BE ASSUMED THAT THE MULES WERE SOLD ALONG WITH IT.**

Rabbi Abahu replied: But we learned in the Mishnah that we *cannot* assume that the mules were sold along with it.

So Rav Tachlifa asked of him: Shall I delete the *baraita*?

Rabbi Abahu answered him: No, explain your *baraita* as referring to a case where the mules are attached to the wagon.

Mishnah: **IF SOMEONE SOLD A YOKE, IT CANNOT BE ASSUMED THAT THE OXEN WERE SOLD ALONG WITH IT. IF SOMEONE SOLD SOME OXEN, IT CANNOT BE ASSUMED THAT THE YOKE WAS SOLD ALONG WITH THEM. RABBI JUDAH SAYS: THE PURCHASE PRICE CAN INDICATE WHAT WAS SOLD.**

Gemara: **What are the circumstances of the case? If the purchase was made in a place where the term "yoke" referred to a yoke alone and the term "oxen" referred to oxen alone, then it is obvious that the yoke was sold and not the oxen, but if the purchase was made in a place where oxen were also included in the term "yoke," then the seller could indeed have sold everything.**

No, it was necessary to state the dispute between Rabbi Judah and the Sages to account for a place where some people used the term "yoke" to refer to a yoke alone and the term "oxen" to refer to oxen alone, while others included oxen in the term "yoke." In such a case, Rabbi Judah was of the opinion that the price could indicate whether oxen were included in the sale, whereas the Sages maintained that the price was no proof.

Chapter Three

Product Liability

Bava Batra 92a–b

הַמּוֹכֵר פֵּירוֹת לַחֲבֵרוֹ וּזְרָעָן וְלֹא צָמְחוּ, וַאֲפִילּוּ זֶרַע פִּשְׁתָּן — אֵינוֹ חַיָּיב בְּאַחֲרָיוּתָן.

רַבָּן שִׁמְעוֹן בֶּן גַּמְלִיאֵל אוֹמֵר: זֵרְעוֹנֵי גִינָה שֶׁאֵינָן נֶאֱכָלִין — חַיָּיב בְּאַחֲרָיוּתָן.

אִתְּמַר: הַמּוֹכֵר שׁוֹר לַחֲבֵירוֹ, וְנִמְצָא נַגְחָן — רַב אָמַר: הֲרֵי זֶה מִקַּח טָעוּת, וּשְׁמוּאֵל אָמַר: יָכוֹל לוֹמַר לוֹ לִשְׁחִיטָה מְכַרְתִּיו לָךְ.

וְלֶיחֱזֵי אִי גַבְרָא דְּזָבֵין לִנְכַסְתָּא — לִנְכַסְתָּא, אִי לִרְדְיָא — לִרְדְיָא!

בְּגַבְרָא דְּזָבֵין לְהָכִי וּלְהָכִי. — וְלֶיחֱזֵי דְּמֵי הֵיכִי נִינְהוּ!

לָא צְרִיכָא, דְּאַיְיקַר בִּישְׂרָא וְקָם בִּדְמֵי רִדְיָא.

אִי הָכִי, לְמַאי נָפְקָא מִינָהּ?

נָפְקָא מִינָהּ לִטְרָחָא.

הֵיכִי דָּמֵי? אִי דְּלֵיכָּא לְאִישְׁתַּלּוּמֵי מִינֵּיהּ — לִיעַכַּב תּוֹרָא בְּזוּזֵיהּ, דְּאָמְרִי אֱינָשֵׁי: מִן מָרֵי רַשׁוָתֵיךְ פָּארֵי אִפְרַע!

לָא צְרִיכָא, דְּאִיכָּא לְאִישְׁתַּלּוּמֵי מִינֵּיהּ.

רַב אָמַר: הֲרֵי זֶה מִקַּח טָעוּת — בָּתַר רוּבָּא אָזְלִינַן, וְרוּבָּא לְרִדְיָא זָבְנִי; וּשְׁמוּאֵל אָמַר לָךְ: כִּי אָזְלִינַן בָּתַר רוּבָּא — בְּאִיסּוּרָא, בְּמָמוֹנָא — לָא.

Mishnah: **IF ONE PERSON SELLS GRAIN TO ANOTHER, AND THE BUYER PLANTS IT, BUT IT DOES NOT GROW, EVEN IF IT WAS FLAX SEED, WHICH IS USUALLY USED FOR PLANTING, THE SELLER IS NOT LIABLE FOR THE LOSS.**

RABBAN SIMEON BEN GAMALIEL SAYS: FOR GARDEN SEEDS, WHICH ARE NOT EATEN, THE SELLER IS LIABLE FOR THE LOSS.

The Mishnah thus rules that when someone sells grain, expecting the buyer to use his purchase for eating, and the buyer uses it for planting, the seller is not liable for any loss. This ruling is maintained even in the case of flax seed, which is known to be used mostly for planting.

> ## What's Your Opinion?
> Is this ruling of the Mishnah reasonable? If flax seed is usually used for planting, shouldn't a vendor be held liable if a buyer plants the seeds and the flax does not grow? How can the ruling of the Mishnah be justified?

The Gemara questions the logic of this ruling by citing the case of an ox: **It was stated: If one person sells an ox to another and it was found to be a gorer, Rav says: This was a sale made in error,** and the seller must refund to the buyer his money, **but Samuel says: The seller can say to the buyer: I sold it to you for slaughtering,** thus, even though the ox cannot be used for plowing, it still has value as meat, and the sale is not canceled.

The Gemara then questions the circumstances behind the dispute between Rav and Samuel. **Let us see who the buyer is. If it is a person who usually buys for slaughtering, then we can assume that the purchase was intended for slaughtering,** and Rav should agree that the sale is valid. **If it is a person who usually buys for plowing, then we can assume that the purchase was intended for plowing,** and Samuel should agree

Rabban Simeon ben Gamaliel (II), a descendant of Hillel, was a young man during the time of the Bar Kochba revolt (132–135 C.E.) against Rome. After crushing the revolt, the Romans killed many of the leading rabbis and scholars of the period. Rabban Simeon had to go into hiding and was, for a period of time, unable to participate in the work of the scholars. When the persecution decreased, Rabban Simeon joined his colleagues and was appointed *nasi,* president of the Sanhedrin, thus continuing the chain of the presidency in the family of Hillel. His son, Judah, who followed him as *nasi,* compiled the Mishnah. Over a hundred of Rabban Simeon's rulings are recorded in the Mishnah.

Rav and Samuel lived in Palestine for many years and studied with Rabbi Judah HaNasi, the editor of the Mishnah. Rav returned to Babylonia in the year 219 C.E. and there founded a school at Sura, which became a center of Jewish learning for centuries to come. Samuel headed the academy at Nehardea. The two of them became the leading Sages in the first generation of the amoraic period. They often had differences of opinion on legal matters and their controversies are recorded throughout the Talmud. Rav's rulings on matters of ritual law were considered authoritative. Samuel was recognized as the expert in civil law.

that the sale should be canceled. In either case, there should be no dispute between Rav and Samuel.

The Gemara responds: **The dispute between Rav and Samuel has to do with a person who buys both for slaughtering and for plowing.** Thus, in this case, learning the identity of the purchaser does not help in deciding whether the sale is valid.

The Gemara makes another suggestion to show that the dispute between Rav and Samuel was unnecessary: **Let us see what the purchase price was.** An ox that can plow should be worth far more than one that needs to be slaughtered. From the price, then, it would be possible to tell what the purpose of the purchase was.

The Gemara replies: **No. The dispute between Rav and Samuel has to do with a case where the price of meat has risen and is equal to the price of an ox that plows,** so that the purchase price gives no indication as to why the ox was bought.

The Gemara then asks: **If so, why does it matter whether the sale is canceled or not?** Since the buyer will receive the same amount of money having the animal slaughtered as by obtaining a refund from the seller, why does it matter whether or not the sale is canceled?

The Gemara answers: **There is the inconvenience of having to sell the ox.** If the sale is canceled, as Rav rules, the buyer simply gets his money back. If the sale is valid, as Samuel rules, the buyer has to go to the trouble of selling the ox.

The Gemara questions this response: **What is the situation? If the seller has no money from which the buyer can collect a refund, then let the buyer keep the ox in place of the money, as people say, "From your debtor, accept even bran as payment."** Thus even if the sale is canceled, the buyer will still have to go to the trouble of selling the ox. So what difference does it make whether or not the sale is canceled?

The Gemara replies: **No. The dispute matters in a case where the seller has the money from which the buyer can collect a refund.** In such a case, if the sale is canceled because it was made in error, the buyer would not have to go to the trouble of selling the ox.

Having settled the question as to the circumstances behind the dispute, the Gemara proceeds to explain the reason for the opposing rulings of Rav and Samuel: **Rav says that it is a sale made in error because we rule in accordance with the practice of the majority, and the majority of oxen are purchased for plowing. And Samuel says that we rule in accordance with the practice of the majority in matters of ritual prohibitions but not in monetary matters.** Samuel would agree that if there were a doubt about the source of a certain piece of meat, and of the ten butchers in a town, nine were kosher, it could be assumed that the meat was kosher. In monetary matters, however, Samuel stood by the principle that a claimant should not be given a defendant's money without clear proof. "Most people" is not proof in Samuel's view.

What's Your Opinion?

Do you favor the opinion of Rav or of Samuel? If a buyer uses a product the way most people use it, should a merchant be required to void the sale and repay the buyer if the purchase failed to work properly? If a buyer uses a product in an unusual way and it doesn't work properly, is the buyer entitled to a refund? Suppose the seller believed that the buyer planned to use the product in such a way that it would have worked properly, would the sale still have to be rescinded?

Consider This Case

Jon went looking for a car at Mike's Used Car Lot in Seattle. Mike said that he had a well-running eight-year-old Ford with 80,000 miles on the odometer. He recommended it to Jon. Jon bought it for $1,500. A week later, Jon drove his "new" car to San Francisco. On his way home, the car died. The engine burned out and would have cost more than $2,500 to repair. Jon left the car in northern California and returned home by bus.

The next day he went to Mike and demanded a refund. He explained that he had owned the car less than two weeks and had driven it less than 2,000 miles. Mike refused to give Jon his money back, telling Jon that he thought such a car was purchased for local driving and not for a long highway trip.

Do you think that Mike should repay Jon?

תָּא שְׁמַע: הַמּוֹכֵר פֵּירוֹת לַחֲבֵרוֹ וּזְרָעָן וְלֹא צָמְחוּ, וַאֲפִילוּ
זֶרַע פִּשְׁתָּן – אֵינוֹ חַיָּיב בְּאַחֲרָיוּתָן.

מַאי "אֲפִילוּ"? לָאו אֲפִילוּ זֶרַע פִּשְׁתָּן דְּרוּבָּא לִזְרִיעָה זָבְנִי,
וַאֲפִילוּ הָכִי לָא אָזְלִינַן בָּתַר רוּבָּא?

תַּנָּאֵי הִיא; דְּתַנְיָא: הַמּוֹכֵר פֵּירוֹת לַחֲבֵרוֹ וּזְרָעָן וְלֹא צָמְחוּ;
זֵרְעוֹנֵי גִינָּה שֶׁאֵין נֶאֱכָלִין – חַיָּיב בְּאַחֲרָיוּתָן, זֶרַע פִּשְׁתָּן
– אֵינוֹ חַיָּיב בְּאַחֲרָיוּתָן.

רַבִּי יוֹסֵי אוֹמֵר: נוֹתֵן לוֹ דְּמֵי זֶרַע.

The Gemara now cites our own Mishnah to refute Rav and to support Samuel's position: **Come and hear in the Mishnah: IF ONE PERSON SELLS GRAIN TO ANOTHER, AND THE BUYER PLANTS IT, BUT IT DOES NOT GROW, EVEN IF IT WAS FLAX SEED, WHICH IS USUALLY USED FOR PLANTING, THE SELLER IS NOT LIABLE FOR THE LOSS.**

Now what is the significance of the word "even"? Is it not to teach that even in the case of flax seed, which is purchased mostly for planting, even in such a case, we do not rule in accordance with the practice of the majority? The Mishnah explicitly rejects the idea that the seller is liable because most people use the product in the way that the buyer used it. This refutes Rav's position that since most people use a product in a certain way, the seller should pay if it doesn't work when used in that way.

The Gemara admits that our Mishnah successfully refutes Rav, but it cites another tannaitic passage, which supports Rav: **This is a dispute among *Tannaim*. For it was taught in a *baraita*: IF ONE PERSON SELLS GRAIN TO ANOTHER, AND THE BUYER PLANTS IT, AND IT DOES NOT GROW, IF THEY WERE GARDEN SEEDS, WHICH ARE NOT EATEN, THE SELLER IS LIABLE FOR THE LOSS. IF IT WAS FLAX SEED, THE SELLER IS NOT LIABLE FOR THE LOSS.**

RABBI YOSE SAYS: THE SELLER MUST GIVE BACK TO THE BUYER THE MONEY PAID FOR THE FLAX SEED.

Rabbi Yose ben Chalafta, who is usually cited in the Mishnah simply as Rabbi Yose, was one of Rabbi Akiva's major students. Because of persecution by the Romans, his rabbinic ordination had to take place in secret. After his ordination, to avoid the Romans, he fled to Asia Minor and remained there until the persecution decreased. Then he returned to Palestine and took an active part in the work of the academy. His rulings are included throughout the Mishnah and in many *baraitot*. His opinions were so well respected that the law generally followed his views.

The Gemara thus shows that even though our Mishnah and the anonymous *Tanna* of this *baraita* support the view of Samuel, there was a *Tanna*, Rabbi Yose, who maintained that since most people used flax seed for planting, the seller was liable for the loss. In other words, Rabbi Yose held that we rule in accordance with the practice of the majority, just as Rav taught. In this way, the Gemara shows that the dispute between Rav and Samuel is a reflection of a dispute in tannaitic times.

Bava Batra 93b

תָּנוּ רַבָּנָן: מַהוּ נוֹתֵן לוֹ? דְּמֵי זֶרַע וְלֹא הוֹצָאָה, וְיֵשׁ אוֹמְרִים: אַף הוֹצָאָה.

מַאן ״יֵשׁ אוֹמְרִים״? אָמַר רַב חִסְדָּא: רַבָּן שִׁמְעוֹן בֶּן גַּמְלִיאֵל הִיא.

Rav Chisda was a Babylonian *Amora* whose life spanned most of the third century and the beginning of the fourth century. He is one of the most frequently mentioned Sages in the Babylonian Talmud and is also often cited in the Jerusalem Talmud. In the last decade of his life, he became head of the academy at Sura. Early in his life he was poor, but later, working as a brewer, he became wealthy. It is reported that when the academy at Sura fell into disrepair, he rebuilt it at his own expense.

In the Mishnah, Rabban Simeon ben Gamaliel had stated that if garden seeds, which were used only for planting, failed in their purpose, the seller was liable for the loss. The question arose as to whether the seller was liable only for the cost of the seeds, or liable also for the expenses incurred by the buyer in planting the faulty seeds. The Gemara explores the extent of the seller's liability: **The Rabbis have taught in a *baraita*: WHAT DOES A SELLER WHO IS LIABLE FOR LOSS HAVE TO PAY THE BUYER? THE COST OF THE SEEDS, BUT NOT FOR EXPENSES IN PLANTING THEM. BUT THERE ARE SOME WHO SAY: EVEN FOR THE EXPENSES.**

The Gemara asks: **To whom does the *baraita* refer when it says: THERE ARE SOME WHO SAY? Rav Chisda says: It is Rabban Simeon ben Gamaliel.**

Bava Batra 93b

דְּתַנְיָא: הַמּוֹלִיךְ חִטִּין לִטְחוֹן, וְלֹא לְתָתָן, וַעֲשָׂאָן סוּבִּין אוֹ מוּרְסָן. קֶמַח לַנַּחְתּוֹם, וַאֲפָאוֹ פַּת נִיפּוֹלִין. בְּהֵמָה לַטַּבָּח, וְנִיבְּלָהּ — חַיָּיב, מִפְּנֵי שֶׁהוּא כְּנוֹשֵׂא שָׂכָר.

רַבָּן שִׁמְעוֹן בֶּן גַּמְלִיאֵל אוֹמֵר: נוֹתֵן לוֹ דְּמֵי בּוֹשְׁתּוֹ וּדְמֵי בּוֹשֶׁת אוֹרְחָיו.

וְכֵן הָיָה רַבָּן שִׁמְעוֹן בֶּן גַּמְלִיאֵל אוֹמֵר: מִנְהַג גָּדוֹל הָיָה בִּירוּשָׁלַיִם, הַמּוֹסֵר סְעוּדָה לַחֲבֵרוֹ וְקִלְקְלָהּ — נוֹתֵן לוֹ דְּמֵי בָשְׁתּוֹ וּדְמֵי בוֹשֶׁת אוֹרְחָיו.

For it was taught in a *baraita:* **IF SOMEONE TAKES WHEAT TO A MILLER AND THE MILLER DOES NOT MOISTEN IT BEFORE GRINDING IT AND MAKES IT INTO COARSE BRAN OR BRUISED GRAIN, OR IF SOMEONE TAKES FLOUR TO A BAKER AND THE BAKER MAKES IT INTO CRUMBLY BREAD, OR IF SOMEONE TAKES AN ANIMAL TO A BUTCHER AND THE BUTCHER RENDERS IT UNFIT FOR EATING, THE BUSINESS OWNER IS LIABLE—BEING LIKE A PAID GUARDIAN [OF GOODS, RESPONSIBLE FOR ANY DAMAGE TO THEM].**

RABBAN SIMEON BEN GAMALIEL SAYS: THE BUSINESS OWNER MUST ALSO PAY FOR THE CUSTOMER'S EMBARRASSMENT AND FOR THE EMBARRASSMENT OF THE CUSTOMER'S GUESTS.

The Gemara cites this *baraita* to make a point: If Rabban Simeon ben Gamaliel holds a business owner who spoils a product liable for the embarrassment caused a customer, then he surely holds one who sells seeds that will not grow liable for the actual expenses a customer incurred.

The Gemara then provides a second *baraita,* which makes the same point: **AND THUS DID RABBAN SIMEON BEN GAMALIEL SAY: THERE WAS A GREAT CUSTOM IN JERUSALEM: IF ONE HIRED SOMEONE ELSE TO PREPARE A BANQUET, WHO THEN RUINED IT, THE PREPARER HAD TO PAY FOR THE EMBARRASSMENT CAUSED TO THE HOST AND FOR THE EMBARRASSMENT CAUSED TO THE GUESTS.** Again Rabban Simeon ben Gamaliel rules that one who ruins a product has to pay for the resulting embarrassment. This strengthens the view that Rabban Simeon ben Gamaliel was the one who held that a seller of seeds that don't grow is liable for the cost of the seeds and for the expenses incurred in planting them.

What's Your Opinion?

In your opinion, can we deduce, as the Gemara does, that Rabban Simeon ben Gamaliel was of the opinion that a vendor who was guilty of making a sale in error had to refund the buyer's money and reimburse incurred expenses (labor, fertilizer, etc.) as well? Do you agree with the view that the seller of a faulty product must not only refund the cost of the product, but also pay for any expenses incurred?

Consider This Case

Best's Batteries sold a thousand batteries to the Terrific Toy Company. Some of the batteries leaked, and a number of toys were ruined, causing expense to the toy company and damage to its reputation. Which of the following costs do you think Best's Batteries should have to cover?

1. Replacement of faulty batteries.
2. Replacement of damaged toys.
3. Damage to the toy company's reputation.
4. Other.

R E V I E W I N G   T H E   T E X T

Bava Batra 92a–b

Mishnah: **IF ONE PERSON SELLS GRAIN TO ANOTHER, AND THE BUYER PLANTS IT, BUT IT DOES NOT GROW, EVEN IF IT WAS FLAX SEED, WHICH IS USUALLY USED FOR PLANTING, THE SELLER IS NOT LIABLE FOR THE LOSS.**

RABBAN SIMEON BEN GAMALIEL SAYS: FOR GARDEN SEEDS, WHICH ARE NOT EATEN, THE SELLER IS LIABLE FOR THE LOSS.

Gemara: **It was stated: If one person sells an ox to another and it was found to be a gorer, Rav says: This was a sale made in error, but Samuel says: The seller can say to the buyer: I sold it to you for slaughtering.**

Let us see who the buyer is. If it is a person who usually buys for slaughtering, then we can assume that the

purchase was intended for slaughtering. If it is a person who usually buys for plowing, then we can assume that the purchase was intended for plowing.

The dispute between Rav and Samuel has to do with a person who buys both for slaughtering and for plowing.

Let us see what the purchase price was.

No. The dispute between Rav and Samuel has to do with a case where the price of meat has risen and is equal to the price of an ox that plows.

If so, why does it matter whether the sale is canceled or not?

There is the inconvenience of having to sell the ox.

What is the situation? If the seller has no money from which the buyer can collect a refund, then let the buyer keep the ox in place of the money, as people say, "From your debtor, accept even bran as payment."

No. The dispute matters in a case where the seller has the money from which the buyer can collect a refund.

Rav says that it is a sale made in error because we rule in accordance with the practice of the majority, and the majority of oxen are purchased for plowing. And Samuel says that we rule in accordance with the practice of the majority in matters of ritual prohibitions but not in monetary matters.

Bava Batra 93a–b

Gemara: **Come and hear in the Mishnah: IF ONE PERSON SELLS GRAIN TO ANOTHER, AND THE BUYER PLANTS IT, BUT IT DOES NOT GROW, EVEN IF IT WAS FLAX SEED, WHICH IS USUALLY USED FOR PLANTING, THE SELLER IS NOT LIABLE FOR THE LOSS.**

Now what is the significance of the word "even"? Is it not to teach that even in the case of flax seed, which is purchased mostly for planting, even in such a case, we do not rule in accordance with the practice of the majority.

This is a dispute among *Tannaim*. For it was taught in a *baraita:* IF ONE PERSON SELLS GRAIN TO ANOTHER, AND THE BUYER PLANTS IT, AND IT DOES NOT GROW, IF THEY WERE GARDEN SEEDS, WHICH ARE NOT EATEN, THE SELLER IS LIABLE FOR THE LOSS. IF IT WAS FLAX SEED, THE SELLER IS NOT LIABLE FOR THE LOSS.

RABBI YOSE SAYS: THE SELLER MUST GIVE BACK TO THE BUYER THE MONEY PAID FOR THE FLAX SEED.

Bava Batra 93b

Gemara: **The Rabbis have taught in a *baraita:*** WHAT DOES A SELLER WHO IS LIABLE FOR LOSS HAVE TO PAY THE BUYER? THE COST OF THE SEEDS, BUT NOT FOR EXPENSES IN PLANTING THEM. BUT THERE ARE SOME WHO SAY: EVEN FOR THE EXPENSES.

To whom does the *baraita* refer when it says: THERE ARE SOME WHO SAY? **Rav Chisda says: It is Rabban Simeon ben Gamaliel.**

Bava Batra 93b

Gemara: **For it was taught in a *baraita:*** IF SOMEONE TAKES WHEAT TO A MILLER AND THE MILLER DOES NOT MOISTEN IT BEFORE GRINDING IT AND MAKES IT INTO COARSE BRAN OR BRUISED GRAIN, OR IF SOMEONE TAKES FLOUR TO A BAKER AND THE BAKER MAKES IT INTO CRUMBLY BREAD, OR IF SOMEONE TAKES AN ANIMAL TO A BUTCHER AND THE BUTCHER RENDERS IT UNFIT FOR EATING, THE BUSINESS OWNER IS LIABLE—BEING LIKE A PAID GUARDIAN [OF GOODS, RESPONSIBLE FOR ANY DAMAGE TO THEM].

RABBAN SIMEON BEN GAMALIEL SAYS: THE BUSINESS OWNER MUST ALSO PAY FOR THE CUSTOMER'S EMBARRASSMENT AND FOR THE EMBARRASSMENT OF THE CUSTOMER'S GUESTS.

AND THUS DID RABBAN SIMEON BEN GAMALIEL SAY: THERE WAS A GREAT CUSTOM IN JERUSALEM: IF ONE HIRED SOMEONE ELSE TO PREPARE A BANQUET, WHO THEN RUINED IT, THE PREPARER HAD TO PAY FOR THE EMBARRASSMENT CAUSED TO THE HOST AND FOR THE EMBARRASSMENT CAUSED TO THE GUESTS.

Chapter Four

Allowing for Imperfection

Bava Batra 93b

הַמּוֹכֵר פֵּירוֹת לַחֲבֵירוֹ — הֲרֵי זֶה מְקַבֵּל עָלָיו רוֹבַע טְנוֹפֶת לִסְאָה; תְּאֵנִים — מְקַבֵּל עָלָיו עֶשֶׂר מְתוּלָעוֹת לְמֵאָה; מַרְתֵּף שֶׁל יַיִן — מְקַבֵּל עָלָיו עֶשֶׂר קוֹסְסוֹת לְמֵאָה; קַנְקַנִּים בַּשָּׁרוֹן — מְקַבֵּל עָלָיו עֶשֶׂר פִּיטָסוֹת לְמֵאָה.

Mishnah: **IF ONE PERSON SELLS GRAIN TO ANOTHER, THE BUYER MUST BE WILLING TO ACCEPT A QUARTER OF A *KAV* OF BAD GRAIN PER *SEAH*. AS FOR FIGS, THE BUYER MUST BE WILLING TO ACCEPT TEN WORMY ONES PER HUNDRED. AS FOR A WINE CELLAR, THE BUYER MUST BE WILLING TO ACCEPT TEN JARS OF SOURISH WINE PER HUNDRED. AS FOR JUGS BOUGHT IN SHARON, THE BUYER MUST BE WILLING TO ACCEPT TEN FAULTY ONES PER HUNDRED.**

A *kav* is one-sixth of a *seah*; thus, if no more than one-twenty-fourth of the grain is spoiled, the grain will still be acceptable.

Bava Batra 94a

אָמַר רַב הוּנָא: אִם בָּא לְנַפּוֹת — מְנַפֶּה אֶת כּוּלוֹ.

אָמְרִי לַהּ: דִּינָא, וְאָמְרִי לַהּ: קְנָסָא.

אָמְרִי לַהּ דִּינָא: מַאן דְּיָהֵיב זוּזֵי — אַפֵּירֵי שַׁפִּירֵי יָהֵיב, וְרוֹבַע לָא טָרַח אִינִישׁ, יוֹתֵר מֵרוֹבַע טָרַח אִינִישׁ, וְכֵיוָן דְּטָרַח — טָרַח בְּכוּלֵּיהּ.

Rav Huna, a Babylonian *Amora* of the third century, was the foremost student of Rav. When his master died, Rav Huna became head of the academy at Sura, a position he held for some forty years. He attracted students from far and wide, often supporting them at his own expense. Early in life he was poor; later, when he attained wealth, he became known for his many charitable works. Through his teaching and his enormous impact on his students, he helped to make Sura the outstanding place of learning that it became and remained for centuries.

וְאָמְרִי לָהּ קְנָסָא: רוֹבַע שְׁכִיחַ, יוֹתֵר לָא שְׁכִיחַ, וְאִיהוּ הוּא דְּעָרֵיב, וְכֵיוָן דְּעָרֵיב — קְנָסוּהוּ רַבָּנַן בְּכוּלֵּיהּ.

Gemara: **Rav Huna said: A buyer who wishes to sift the grain being purchased (to see if it contains more bad grain than is permitted), may sift all of it,** and if in so doing finds more bad grain than is allowed, the seller must make reimbursement for all of the bad grain found, even the bad grain that would normally be allowed.

The Gemara now calls attention to two theories that explain the reason for Rav Huna's ruling: **Some say that Rav Huna's ruling is simply based on the law, while others say that it reflects a penalty imposed on the seller by the Rabbis.**

Some say that it is based on the law, for someone who pays money for grain expects to receive all good grain, but for a quarter of a *kav,* a person doesn't go to the trouble of sifting to remove the bad grain for reimbursement. But for more than a quarter of a *kav,* a person will go to the trouble of sifting. And having gone to the trouble of sifting, the buyer sifts all of the grain and is entitled to be reimbursed for all of the bad grain.

And some say that Rav Huna's ruling reflects a penalty imposed on the seller by the Rabbis. A quarter of a *kav* of bad grain is normal, and we do not presume that the seller intentionally mixed in the bad grain that is found; but more than a quarter of a *kav* of bad grain is not normal, and in such a case, we presume that the seller must have intentionally mixed in the bad grain with good. And since the seller mixed in some of the bad grain, the Rabbis imposed a penalty by requiring reimbursement for all of the bad grain, even that part that is normally permitted.

What's Your Opinion?

Do you agree with Rav Huna's ruling? If not, why not? If you do agree with his ruling, which basis for his ruling do you prefer?

תָּא שְׁמַע: שְׁנַיִם שֶׁהִפְקִידוּ אֵצֶל אֶחָד, זֶה מָנֶה וְזֶה מָאתַיִם, זֶה אוֹמֵר "מָאתַיִם שֶׁלִּי" וְזֶה אוֹמֵר "מָאתַיִם שֶׁלִּי" — נוֹתֵן לָזֶה מָנֶה וְלָזֶה מָנֶה, וְהַשְּׁאָר יְהֵא מוּנָּח עַד שֶׁיָּבֹא אֵלִיָּהוּ!

הָכִי הָשְׁתָּא?! הָתָם וַדַּאי מָנֶה לְמָר וּמָנֶה לְמָר, הָכָא מִי יֵימַר דְּלָאו כּוּלֵּיהּ עֲרוּבֵי עָרִיב?

תָּא שְׁמַע מִסֵּיפָא, אָמַר רַבִּי יוֹסֵי: אִם כֵּן מָה הִפְסִיד הָרַמַּאי? אֶלָּא הַכֹּל יְהֵא מוּנָּח עַד שֶׁיָּבֹא אֵלִיָּהוּ!

הָכִי הָשְׁתָּא?! הָתָם וַדַּאי אִיכָּא רַמַּאי, הָכָא מִי יֵימַר דַּעֲרוּבֵי עָרִיב?

תָּא שְׁמַע: שְׁטָר שֶׁיֵּשׁ בּוֹ רִבִּית — קוֹנְסִין אוֹתוֹ, וְאֵינוֹ גּוֹבֶה לֹא אֶת הַקֶּרֶן וְלֹא אֶת הָרִבִּית, דִּבְרֵי רַבִּי מֵאִיר!

הָכִי הָשְׁתָּא?! הָתָם מִשְׁעַת כְּתִיבָה הוּא דַּעֲבַד לֵיהּ שׁוּמָא, הָכָא מִי יֵימַר דַּעֲרוּבֵי עָרִיב?

תָּא שְׁמַע מִסֵּיפָא, וַחֲכָמִים אוֹמְרִים: גּוֹבֶה אֶת הַקֶּרֶן וְאֵינוֹ גּוֹבֶה אֶת הָרִבִּית!

הָכִי הָשְׁתָּא?! הָתָם וַדַּאי קַרְנָא דְּהֶתֵּירָא הוּא, הָכָא מִי יֵימַר דְּכוּלֵּיהּ לָא עֲרוּבֵי עָרִיב.

The Gemara now seeks to refute Rav Huna's ruling from a Mishnah: **Come and hear: IF TWO PEOPLE DEPOSIT MONEY WITH SOMEONE, ONE OF THEM DEPOSITING A MANEH AND THE OTHER 200 ZUZ, AND WHEN THEY COME TO CLAIM THEIR DEPOSIT, ONE SAYS, "THE 200 ARE MINE," AND THE OTHER ONE SAYS, THE 200 ARE MINE," THE GUARDIAN GIVES THIS ONE A *MANEH* AND THAT ONE A *MANEH,* AND THE REST REMAINS WITH THE GUARDIAN UNTIL ELIJAH COMES.** In this case, the depositor who falsely claimed having deposited 200 *zuz* gets back the *maneh* that was deposited and suffers no penalty for this misdeed. This seems to contradict Rav Huna's ruling in which the seller who included too much bad grain in his sale is penalized by being required to replace not only the excess bad grain, but even the bad grain that is normally allowed.

The Bible does not tell of Elijah's death, only that he rose to heaven in a chariot of fire (2 Kings 2:11). According to tradition, he will return one day, announce the advent of the Messiah, and resolve all disputes and difficulties.

A *maneh* equals 100 *zuz*.

The Gemara now rejects this analogy: **How can you compare these two cases? There, in the case of the Mishnah, a *maneh* certainly belongs to this one and to that one. Here, however, in the case of an excess amount of bad grain, who is to say that the seller did not mix in all of the bad grain personally?** In the case of the Mishnah, the cheater who wanted to obtain an extra *maneh* did, without question, deposit one *maneh*. But in the case of the sale of grain, it is possible that the seller inserted the bad grain intentionally—not only the excess bad grain, but even the part that is normally overlooked.

Failing in its attempt to refute Rav Huna's ruling, the Gemara seeks to confirm Rav Huna's ruling from the continuation of the same Mishnah: **Come and hear from the ending part of the Mishnah: RABBI YOSE SAID: IF SO, IF EACH DEPOSITOR GETS BACK A *MANEH*, THEN WHAT DOES THE CHEATER LOSE? RATHER, ALL OF THE MONEY SHOULD REMAIN WITH THE GUARDIAN UNTIL ELIJAH COMES.** Thus, Rabbi Yose's view, that in order to discourage cheating even that portion of the deposit that is not under dispute should be withheld, lends support to Rav Huna's ruling that, because we believe that the seller may have intentionally mixed in the bad grain, we penalize him and require him to take back even the permitted amount of bad grain.

The Gemara also rejects this analogy: **How can you compare these two cases? There, in the case of the Mishnah,** where two depositors each claim to be the one who deposited two *maneh*s, **there is definitely a cheater involved. Here, however, in the case of an excess amount of bad grain, who can say for sure that the seller mixed in any bad grain?**

The Gemara again seeks to find support for Rav Huna's ruling, this time from a *baraita*: **Come and hear: IN THE CASE OF A PROMISSORY NOTE THAT INCLUDES A PROVISION FOR THE PAYMENT OF INTEREST, WE PENALIZE THE LENDER, WHO MAY COLLECT NEITHER THE PRINCIPAL NOR THE INTEREST. THESE ARE THE WORDS OF RABBI MEIR.** Thus Rabbi Meir, who would penalize the lender in such a case by prohibiting him from collecting even the permitted portion of the loan, lends support to Rav Huna's ruling that where an excess of bad grain is discovered, the seller is penalized by being

Lending on interest is forbidden in the Bible (Deut. 23:20). The law was established for the protection of the poor. If people were so poor that they had to seek a loan, it was considered wrong to take advantage of this condition by requiring them to pay back more than they had borrowed. Talmudic law reinforces this prohibition.

Rabbi Meir, who lived in the middle of the second century, was one of the principal students of Rabbi Akiva. Because of persecutions by the Romans that followed the Bar Kochba revolt (132–135 C.E.), he had to flee from Palestine for a period of time. After the persecutions subsided, he returned to his work and was among the Sages who gathered at Usha to renew the work of the Sanhedrin. He played a critical role in organizing and editing the law in his time. When Rabbi Judah HaNasi, in the next generation, compiled the Mishnah, he relied to a great extent on the work of Rabbi Meir. It is, in fact, believed that the anonymous statements in the Mishnah express the viewpoint of Rabbi Meir. Rabbi Meir's wife, Beruriyah, was a scholar in her own right.

required to take back not only the excess bad grain, but the permitted bad grain as well.

The Gemara rejects the proof: **How can you compare these two cases? There, in the case of the promissory note, at the moment the note was written, the lender imposed a forbidden interest charge on the borrower. Here, however, who can say for sure that the seller mixed in any bad grain with the good grain?**

Based on the second part of the same *baraita,* the Gemara now seeks to refute Rav Huna's ruling: **Come and hear from the ending part of the *baraita:* BUT THE SAGES SAY: THE LENDER MAY COLLECT THE PRINCIPAL BUT NOT THE INTEREST.** The Sages do not penalize the lender for having sought to charge interest on the loan. This refutes Rav Huna's view that we apply a penalty by requiring the seller to take back even the permitted amount of bad grain.

The Gemara rejects this refutation as well: **How can you compare these two cases? There, in the case of the promissory note, it is certain that the principal is permitted. Here, however, who is to say that the seller did not mix in all of the bad grain?**

The Gemara is thus unable to find a successful support or a successful refutation of Rav Huna's ruling.

The Gemara often includes arguments that fail to sustain or to refute the matters under discussion. If the only purpose of the Gemara were to determine what the law should be, failed arguments would undoubtedly have been omitted from the text. However, the editors of the Gemara appear to have been more interested in exploring and clarifying legal principles than in merely rendering decisions.

What's Your Opinion?

Should a buyer be required to accept any amount of bad grain with the purchase? If some bad grain is allowable, should it be restricted to a certain percentage? If the allowable percentage is exceeded, should the seller have to replace all of the bad grain, as Rav Huna ruled, or should he have to replace only the bad grain above the acceptable level?

Consider This Case

Philip, the owner of the Main Street Grocery Store, gets his Golden Delicious apples from the local Apple Farm. He likes their apples for their sweet, tangy flavor, and his customers buy them as rapidly as he can supply them.

But the customers at the Main Street Grocery Store are very picky. They don't buy an apple unless it looks perfect or near perfect. Philip knows that not every apple that he gets from the Apple Farm will be perfect. Some will have slight bruises; others will be more seriously damaged. Philip has an arrangement with the Apple Farm. If less than 5 percent of the apples cannot be sold, he will still pay for the entire shipment. Usually the unsold apples amount to only 1 or 2 percent of a delivery, but a recent shipment of 1,000 apples contained 120 bad ones that could not be sold. Philip said that he would pay only for 880 apples. The Apple Farm demanded payment for 950. Who is right?

Bava Batra 97b–98a

הַמּוֹכֵר יַיִן לַחֲבֵירוֹ וְהֶחְמִיץ — אֵינוֹ חַיָּיב בְּאַחֲרָיוּתוֹ, וְאִם יָדוּעַ שֶׁיֵּינוֹ מַחְמִיץ — הֲרֵי זֶה מִקַּח טָעוּת.

וְאִם אָמַר לוֹ: "יַיִן מְבוּשָׂם אֲנִי מוֹכֵר לָךְ" — חַיָּיב לְהַעֲמִיד לוֹ עַד הָעֲצֶרֶת, וְ"יָשָׁן" — מִשֶּׁל אֶשְׁתָּקַד, וּ"מְיוּשָׁן" — מִשֶּׁל שָׁלֹשׁ שָׁנִים.

אָמַר רַבִּי יוֹסֵי בְּרַבִּי חֲנִינָא: לֹא שָׁנוּ אֶלָּא בְּקַנְקַנִּים דְּלוֹקֵחַ, אֲבָל בְּקַנְקַנִּים דְּמוֹכֵר — אָמַר לֵיהּ: הָא חַמְרָךְ וְהָא קַנְקַנָּךְ.

וְכִי קַנְקַנִּין דְּמוֹכֵר מַאי הָוֵי? לֵימָא לֵיהּ: לָא אִיבָּעֵי לָךְ לְשַׁהוּיֵי!

לָא צְרִיכָא, דַּאֲמַר לֵיהּ לְמִקְפָּה.

Mishnah: **IF ONE PERSON SELLS WINE TO ANOTHER AND IT SOURS, THE SELLER IS NOT LIABLE FOR THE LOSS. BUT IF IT IS KNOWN THAT THIS MERCHANT'S WINE SOURS, THEN IT IS A SALE MADE IN ERROR, AND THE SELLER MUST REFUND THE BUYER'S MONEY.**

AND IF IT WAS SAID: I AM SELLING YOU SPICED WINE, THEN THE SELLER IS RESPONSIBLE FOR IT UNTIL SHAVUOT. AND IF IT WAS STATED THAT THE WINE WAS OLD, THEN IT MUST BE FROM THE PREVIOUS YEAR. AND IF IT WAS STATED THAT IT WAS AGED, THEN IT MUST BE FROM THE YEAR BEFORE LAST.

Gemara: **Rabbi Yose bar Chanina said: The law that absolves the seller of liability if the wine sours applies only when the wine was transferred to the buyer's jugs. But if it remained in the seller's jugs, the buyer can say, "Take your wine and take your jug," and the seller must refund the buyer's money.**

The Gemara raises a question: **But even if the wine was left in the seller's jugs, what difference does it make? For the seller could say to the buyer, "You should not have kept the wine for such a long time."** Thus the fault would be with the buyer for having kept the wine too long, and the seller would be absolved from reimbursement.

The Gemara replies: **No, Rabbi Yose bar Chanina's ruling, which holds the seller responsible when the wine remains in its original jugs, is necessary, for it applies in a case where the buyer told the seller of plans to use the wine for cooking,** which means that the seller knew that this wine would be used over a long period of time.

The Gemara thus accepts Rabbi Yose bar Chanina's interpretation of the Mishnah:

1. If the wine is in the buyer's jugs, the seller is exempt.

2. If the wine is in the seller's jugs and the seller is informed that the wine was purchased for cooking (and thus needs to last for a long time), the seller is liable.

3. If the wine is in the seller's jugs and the seller is not informed that the wine was purchased for cooking, the seller is exempt.

Wine mixed with spices is intended to last longer than ordinary wine, at least until the start of summer, around the time of Shavuot.

Shavuot is the Feast of Weeks. It is a harvest festival and a holiday celebrating the giving of the Torah to the people of Israel at Mount Sinai. It comes in the late spring, seven weeks after Passover.

Rabbi Yose bar Chanina was a Palestinian *Amora* of the second half of the third century. He was one of the leading students of Rabbi Yochanan.

What's Your Opinion?

Do you think it is right for the seller to be exempt if the wine sours in the buyer's jugs? Do you think it should matter whether or not the seller is informed as to the purpose of the purchase? In your opinion, how long should a seller be liable for the wine? How long should a seller be liable for milk, bread, a TV, a computer, a car?

Consider This Case

Leah is a caterer; she specializes in bar/bat mitzvah parties and wedding dinners. On one occasion she bought six cases of cottage cheese from a local wholesaler on Tuesday for a wedding dinner the following Sunday. When she opened the containers on the day of the wedding, the cottage cheese was rancid. The next day she demanded a refund from her supplier. He refused, saying that he had sold the cottage cheese before the date stamped on the containers and that she should not have bought such a product five days in advance of its use. Leah replied that refrigerated cottage cheese should last much longer than five days. In your opinion, should Leah be granted a refund?

R E V I E W I N G   T H E   T E X T

Bava Batra 93b

Mishnah: **IF ONE PERSON SELLS GRAIN TO ANOTHER, THE BUYER MUST BE WILLING TO ACCEPT A QUARTER OF A *KAV* OF BAD GRAIN PER *SEAH*. AS FOR FIGS, THE BUYER MUST BE WILLING TO ACCEPT TEN WORMY ONES PER HUNDRED. AS FOR A WINE CELLAR, THE BUYER MUST BE WILLING TO ACCEPT TEN JARS OF SOURISH WINE PER HUNDRED. AS FOR JUGS BOUGHT IN SHARON, THE BUYER MUST BE WILLING TO ACCEPT TEN FAULTY ONES PER HUNDRED.**

Gemara: **Rav Huna said: A buyer who wishes to sift the grain being purchased (to see if it contains more bad grain than is permitted), may sift all of it.**

Some say that Rav Huna's ruling is simply based on the law, while others say that it reflects a penalty imposed on the seller by the Rabbis.

Some say that it is based on the law, for someone who pays money for grain expects to receive all good grain, but for a quarter of a *kav*, a person doesn't go to the trouble of sifting to remove the bad grain for reimbursement. But for more than a quarter of a *kav*, a person will go to the trouble of sifting. And having gone to the trouble of sifting, the buyer sifts all of the grain and is entitled to be reimbursed for all of the bad grain.

And some say that Rav Huna's ruling reflects a penalty imposed on the seller by the Rabbis. A quarter of a *kav* of bad grain is normal, and we do not presume that the seller intentionally mixed in the bad grain that is found; but more than a quarter of a *kav* of bad grain is not normal, and in such a case, we presume that the seller must have intentionally mixed in the bad grain with good. And since the seller mixed in some of the bad grain, the Rabbis imposed a penalty by requiring reimbursement for all of the bad grain, even that part that is normally permitted.

Gemara: **Come and hear: IF TWO PEOPLE DEPOSIT MONEY WITH SOMEONE, ONE OF THEM DEPOSITING A *MANEH* AND THE OTHER 200 *ZUZ*, AND WHEN THEY COME TO CLAIM THEIR DEPOSIT, ONE SAYS, "THE 200 ARE MINE," AND THE OTHER ONE SAYS, "THE 200 ARE MINE," THE GUARDIAN GIVES THIS ONE A *MANEH* AND THAT ONE A *MANEH*, AND THE REST REMAINS WITH THE GUARDIAN UNTIL ELIJAH COMES.**

How can you compare these two cases? There, in the case of the Mishnah, a *maneh* certainly belongs to this one and

to that one. Here, however, in the case of an excess amount of bad grain, who is to say that the seller did not mix in all of the bad grain personally?

Come and hear from the ending part of the Mishnah: RABBI YOSE SAID: IF SO, IF EACH DEPOSITOR GETS BACK A *MANEH,* THEN WHAT DOES THE CHEATER LOSE? RATHER, ALL OF THE MONEY SHOULD REMAIN WITH THE GUARDIAN UNTIL ELIJAH COMES.

How can you compare these two cases? There, in the case of the Mishnah, there is definitely a cheater involved. Here, however, in the case of an excess amount of bad grain, who can say for sure that the seller mixed in any bad grain?

Come and hear: IN THE CASE OF A PROMISSORY NOTE THAT INCLUDES A PROVISION FOR THE PAYMENT OF INTEREST, WE PENALIZE THE LENDER, WHO MAY COLLECT NEITHER THE PRINCIPAL NOR THE INTEREST. THESE ARE THE WORDS OF RABBI MEIR.

How can you compare these two cases? There, in the case of the promissory note, at the moment the note was written, the lender imposed a forbidden interest charge on the borrower. Here, however, who can say for sure that the seller mixed in any bad grain with the good grain?

Come and hear from the ending part of the *baraita:* BUT THE SAGES SAY: THE LENDER MAY COLLECT THE PRINCIPAL BUT NOT THE INTEREST.

How can you compare these two cases? There, in the case of the promissory note, it is certain that the principal is permitted. Here, however, who is to say that the seller did not mix in all of the bad grain?

Bava Batra 97b–98a

Mishnah: IF ONE PERSON SELLS WINE TO ANOTHER AND IT SOURS, THE SELLER IS NOT LIABLE FOR THE LOSS. BUT IF IT IS KNOWN THAT THIS MERCHANT'S WINE SOURS, THEN IT IS A SALE MADE IN ERROR, AND THE SELLER MUST REFUND THE BUYER'S MONEY.

AND IF IT WAS SAID: I AM SELLING YOU SPICED WINE, THEN THE SELLER IS RESPONSIBLE FOR IT UNTIL SHAVUOT. AND IF IT WAS STATED THAT THE WINE WAS OLD, THEN IT MUST BE FROM THE PREVIOUS YEAR. AND IF IT WAS STATED THAT IT WAS AGED, THEN IT MUST BE FROM THE YEAR BEFORE LAST.

Gemara: **Rabbi Yose bar Chanina said: The law that absolves the seller of liability if the wine sours applies only when the wine was transferred to the buyer's jugs. But if it remained in the seller's jugs, the buyer can say, "Take your wine and take your jug," and the seller must refund the buyer's money.**

But even if the wine was left in the seller's jugs, what difference does it make? For the seller could say to the buyer, "You should not have kept the wine for such a long time."

No, Rabbi Yose bar Chanina's ruling, which holds the seller responsible when the wine remains in its original jugs, is necessary, for it applies in a case where the buyer told the seller of plans to use the wine for cooking.

Chapter Five

Overcharging and Underpaying

Bava Metzia 49b

הָאוֹנָאָה אַרְבָּעָה כֶּסֶף מֵעֶשְׂרִים וְאַרְבָּעָה כֶּסֶף לַסֶּלַע, שְׁתוּת לַמִּקָּח.

עַד מָתַי מוּתָּר לְהַחֲזִיר? עַד כְּדֵי שֶׁיַּרְאֶה לַתַּגָּר אוֹ לִקְרוֹבוֹ. הוֹרָה רַבִּי טַרְפוֹן בְּלוּד: הָאוֹנָאָה שְׁמוֹנָה כֶּסֶף מֵעֶשְׂרִים וְאַרְבַּע כֶּסֶף לַסֶּלַע, שְׁלִישׁ לַמִּקָּח.

וְשָׂמְחוּ תַּגָּרֵי לוּד.

אָמַר לָהֶם: כָּל הַיּוֹם מוּתָּר לַחֲזוֹר.

אָמְרוּ לוֹ: יַנִּיחַ לָנוּ רַבִּי טַרְפוֹן בִּמְקוֹמֵינוּ, וְחָזְרוּ לְדִבְרֵי חֲכָמִים.

Mishnah: **AN OVERCHARGE OR AN UNDERPAYMENT OF FOUR SILVER PIECES ON AN ITEM WORTH TWENTY-FOUR SILVER PIECES, WHICH MAKE A SELA, THAT IS, ONE-SIXTH OF THE PURCHASE PRICE, IS CONSIDERED CHEATING.**

AFTER BEING OVERCHARGED, HOW LONG DOES A BUYER HAVE TO RETRACT? AS LONG AS IT TAKES TO SHOW THE ARTICLE TO A MERCHANT OR TO A RELATIVE and thus determine if he was overcharged.

The silver piece referred to was called a *maah*. Twenty-four *maot* equaled one *sela*.

42

RABBI TARFON TAUGHT IN LYDDA: AN OVERCHARGE OR AN UNDERPAYMENT OF EIGHT SILVER PIECES ON AN ITEM WORTH A *SELA*, THAT IS, ONE-THIRD OF THE PURCHASE PRICE, IS CONSIDERED CHEATING.

SO THE MERCHANTS OF LYDDA REJOICED because Rabbi Tarfon allowed a higher overcharge than did the majority of the Sages.

HE SAID TO THEM: A BUYER HAS ALL DAY LONG TO RETRACT, giving buyers more time to determine whether or not they had been overcharged.

THEY SAID TO HIM: LET RABBI TARFON LEAVE US AS WE WERE. AND THEY REVERTED TO FOLLOW THE RULING OF THE SAGES.

Bava Metzia 50b

אָמַר רָבָא, הִלְכְתָא: פָּחוֹת מִשְׁתוּת — נִקְנָה מִקָּח, יוֹתֵר עַל שְׁתוּת — בִּיטּוּל מִקָּח. שְׁתוּת — קָנָה וּמַחֲזִיר אוֹנָאָה, וְזֶה וְזֶה בִּכְדֵי שֶׁיִּרְאֶה לַתַּגָּר אוֹ לִקְרוֹבוֹ.

Gemara: **Rava said: The law is: If there is an overcharge of less than one-sixth, the sale is valid; if it is more than one-sixth, the sale is canceled; if it is exactly one-sixth, the sale is valid, but the seller must refund the overcharge. And in both of the latter two cases, the buyer's time to retract is as long as it takes to show the article to a merchant or to a relative.**

Rabbi Tarfon was a descendant of priests. He was born when the Temple was still in existence and took part in its services. After the fall of the Temple, he met with the Sages at Yavneh and helped lay the foundations for Jewish life without a Temple. He is often mentioned in the Mishnah along with his younger colleague, Rabbi Akiva. Rabbi Tarfon is well known for his saying "It is not incumbent upon you to finish the work, but neither are you free to refrain from it."

What's Your Opinion?

Should overcharging be considered cheating? Shouldn't a merchant be allowed to charge whatever a customer is willing to pay?

> **Consider This Case**
>
> Bert runs a medium-sized neighborhood market. Bert is known for charging more for his products than the larger supermarkets in his area. For example, the average price of Red Delicious apples in Seattle in mid-October is 99¢ a pound, whereas Bert's Market charges $1.49 a pound during the same time period. Some people feel that Bert is a bad person. By charging more than the market rate for his goods, he is taking advantage of the fact that some neighborhood people, especially the elderly, cannot easily get to the larger stores. Bert says that many shoppers prefer his place to other grocery stores and are willing to pay more in order to shop there. Should Bert be considered a cheat for charging 50 percent more than the average?

Bava Metzia 50b–51a

"עַד מָתַי מוּתָּר לְהַחֲזִיר כו'".

אָמַר רַב נַחְמָן: לֹא שָׁנוּ אֶלָּא לוֹקֵחַ, אֲבָל מוֹכֵר — לְעוֹלָם חוֹזֵר.

נֵימָא מְסַיַּיע לֵיהּ, "חָזְרוּ לְדִבְרֵי חֲכָמִים". אִי אָמְרַתְּ בִּשְׁלָמָא מוֹכֵר לְעוֹלָם חוֹזֵר — מִשּׁוּם הָכִי חָזְרוּ. אֶלָּא אִי אָמְרַתְּ מוֹכֵר נַמִי כְּלוֹקֵחַ דָּמֵי — מַאי נָפְקָא לְהוּ מִינָּהּ? כִּי הֵיכִי דְּעָבְדִי לֵיהּ רַבָּנַן תַּקַּנְתָּא לַלּוֹקֵחַ הָכִי נַמִי עָבְדִי לֵיהּ רַבָּנַן תַּקַּנְתָּא לַמּוֹכֵר!

תַּגְּרֵי לוּד לָא שְׁכִיחַ דְּטָעוּ.

אוּשְׁפִּזִיכְנֵיהּ דְּרָמִי בַּר חָמָא זַבֵּין חֲמָרָא וּטְעָה. אַשְׁכְּחֵיהּ דַּהֲוָה עָצֵיב, אָמַר לֵיהּ: אַמַּאי עֲצִיבַתְּ?

אָמַר לֵיהּ: זַבֵּינִי חֲמָרָא וּטְעַאי.

אָמַר לֵיהּ: זִיל הֲדַר בָּךְ.

אָמַר לֵיהּ: הָא שְׁהַאי לִי יוֹתֵר מִכְּדֵי שֶׁאֲרָאֶה לַתַּגָּר אוֹ לִקְרוֹבַי.

44

שְׁדַרְיַיה לְקַמֵּיה דְּרַב נַחְמָן. אֲמַר לֵיה: "לֹא שָׁנוּ אֶלָּא לוֹקֵחַ,
אֲבָל מוֹכֵר – לְעוֹלָם חוֹזֵר.

מַאי טַעְמָא?

לוֹקֵחַ מִקָּחוֹ בְּיָדוֹ, כָּל הֵיכָא דְּאָזֵיל מַחֲוֵי לֵיה, וְאָמְרִי לֵיה
אִי טָעָה אִי לָא טָעָה. מוֹכֵר דְּלָא נָקֵט מִקָּחֵיה בְּיָדֵיה,
עַד דְּמִיתְרַמֵי לֵיה זְבִינְתָּא כְּזַבִינְתֵּיה, וְיָדַע אִי טָעָה וְאִי
לָא טָעָה.

Mishnah: **AFTER BEING OVERCHARGED, HOW LONG DOES A
BUYER HAVE TO RETRACT? AS LONG AS IT TAKES TO SHOW
THE ARTICLE TO A MERCHANT OR TO A RELATIVE.**

Gemara: **Rav Nachman said: This Mishnah, restricting the
time in which one may retract, applies only to a buyer who
was overcharged. However, a seller who was underpaid
may always retract.**

The Gemara then explores to see if Rav Nachman's ruling is
compatible with our Mishnah. **Shall we say that the Mishnah
supports the view of Rav Nachman? For the Mishnah says:
THE MERCHANTS OF LYDDA REVERTED TO FOLLOW THE
RULING OF THE SAGES. Now this is understandable if you say
that a seller may always retract, for then Rabbi Tarfon's
ruling, increasing the time available for retracting, applied
only to buyers, and the merchants reverted to follow the
ruling of the Sages to avoid giving buyers any additional
time. But if you were to say that Rabbi Tarfon's ruling,
increasing the time limit, applied to the seller as well as to
the buyer, then what difference would it make to the
merchants, for the enactment benefiting the buyer would
also benefit the seller?** If the ruling of Rabbi Tarfon to increase
the time available for retracting from a sale applied to sellers as
well as to buyers, then the merchants of Lydda would have
benefited from the ruling as much as the buyers would have, and
they would have had no incentive to revert to follow the ruling of
the Sages. The fact that they did revert to the Sages shows that the
ruling did not apply to sellers, as Rav Nachman taught.

Rav Nachman bar Jacob is
one of the most frequently
mentioned Sages in the
Babylonian Talmud. He lived
during the third and fourth
centuries and is usually just
called Rav Nachman. He was
considered an expert in civil
law, and later generations, as
a rule, followed his opinions.
His foremost disciple was Rava.

The Gemara rejects this argument: **The merchants of Lydda do not often make the mistake of receiving an underpayment.** Thus, even if Rabbi Tarfon's ruling applied to sellers as well as to buyers, there would not be much benefit to the sellers. They would still prefer the ruling of the Sages, which did not give one much time to discover that the sale price was in error. Thus the Mishnah does not serve to support Rav Nachman's ruling.

The Gemara then tells of a time when Rav Nachman put his ruling into practice in the courtroom: **The landlord of Rami bar Chama sold some wine but made a mistake, undercharging the buyer. Rami found him to be sad and said to him, "Why are you sad?"**

He said to him, "I sold some wine and made a mistake."

Rami said to him, "Go and retract."

His landlord replied, "I have delayed longer than the time necessary to show it to a merchant or a relative."

Rami sent him to Rav Nachman, who said to him, "The Mishnah restricting the time in which one may retract applies only to a buyer who was overcharged. However, a seller who was underpaid may always retract."

The Gemara then inquires: **What is the reason for Rav Nachman's ruling that restricts the time allowed to a buyer to retract from a sale but allows a seller an unlimited amount of time?**

The Gemara responds: **The buyer, who has the purchase in hand, goes around and shows it, and people say whether or not the purchase was a mistake. On the other hand, the seller, who does not have the purchase in hand, must wait until coming upon an item like the one sold, and only then can know whether or not the sale was a mistake.** Therefore the seller should not have a time limit on retracting a sale involving underpayment.

Rami bar Chama was a fourth-century Sage. He was known for his brilliance and his independent thinking.

What's Your Opinion?

What's Your Opinion?

If overcharging is to be banned, do you think that there should be a limit as to the amount of time a buyer has to retract a purchase? What do you think should be considered a reasonable amount of time?

Consider This Case

Jerome bought a Picasso lithograph at the Elegant Gallery for $6,000. Edmund, the owner of the gallery, told Jerome that $6,000 was a good price for the picture. Three weeks later, several art experts were at Jerome's house. They informed him that the market price for that particular lithograph was $3,000. Jerome felt that he had been cheated and demanded of Edmund that the sale be rescinded.

Do you think Edmund should be willing to take back the picture and refund Jerome his money?

Bava Metzia 51a

אֶחָד הַלּוֹקֵחַ וְאֶחָד הַמּוֹכֵר יֵשׁ לָהֶן אוֹנָאָה.

כְּשֵׁם שֶׁאוֹנָאָה לַהֶדְיוֹט כָּךְ אוֹנָאָה לַתַּגָּר.

רַבִּי יְהוּדָה אוֹמֵר: אֵין אוֹנָאָה לַתַּגָּר.

מִי שֶׁהוּטַּל עָלָיו יָדוֹ עַל הָעֶלְיוֹנָה, רָצָה — אוֹמֵר לוֹ: תֵּן לִי מְעוֹתַי, אוֹ תֵּן לִי מַה שֶּׁאִנִּיתַנִי.

Mishnah: **THE LAW AGAINST CHEATING APPLIES BOTH TO A BUYER WHO IS OVERCHARGED AND TO A SELLER WHO IS UNDERPAID.**

JUST AS THE LAW AGAINST CHEATING APPLIES TO AN ORDINARY PERSON WHO IS OVERCHARGED, SO IT APPLIES TO A MERCHANT WHO IS UNDERPAID.

RABBI JUDAH SAYS: THE LAW AGAINST CHEATING DOES NOT APPLY TO A MERCHANT WHO IS UNDERPAID.

WHOEVER IS CHEATED HAS THE ADVANTAGE: A BUYER WHO IS CHEATED MAY SAY EITHER: GIVE ME BACK MY MONEY, OR GIVE ME BACK THE AMOUNT BY WHICH YOU CHEATED ME. Thus, a buyer who was overcharged has the option of either canceling the sale and getting a full refund or of receiving a refund for the amount overcharged; and a seller who was underpaid has the option of either canceling the sale and getting back what was sold or of receiving a payment of the amount underpaid.

Bava Metzia 51a

רַבִּי יְהוּדָה אוֹמֵר: אֵין אוֹנָאָה לַתַּגָּר.

מִשּׁוּם שֶׁהוּא תַּגָּר אֵין לוֹ אוֹנָאָה?

אָמַר רַב נַחְמָן אָמַר רַב: בְּתַגָּר סַפְסָר שָׁנוּ. מַאי טַעְמָא — מֵידַע יָדַע זְבִינָתֵיה כַּמָּה שַׁוְיָא, וְאַחוּלֵי אַחֵיל גַּבֵּיה. וְהַאי דְזַבְּנָא הָכִי — מִשּׁוּם דְּאִתְרְמְיָא לֵיה זְבִינְתָּא אַחֲרִיתִי. — וְהַשְׁתָּא מִיהָא קָא הָדַר בֵּיה!

רַב אַשִׁי אֲמַר: מַאי אֵין לַתַּגָּר אוֹנָאָה — אֵינוֹ בְּתוֹרַת אוֹנָאָה, שֶׁאֲפִילוּ פָּחוֹת מִכְּדֵי אוֹנָאָה חוֹזֵר.

תַּנְיָא כְּוָותֵיה דְרַב נַחְמָן, רַבִּי יְהוּדָה אוֹמֵר: תַּגָּר אֵין לוֹ אוֹנָאָה, מִפְּנֵי שֶׁהוּא בָּקִי.

The Mishnah stated: **RABBI JUDAH SAYS: THE LAW AGAINST CHEATING DOES NOT APPLY TO A MERCHANT WHO IS UNDERPAID.**

The Gemara questions Rabbi Judah's opinion: **Is it right that by virtue of being a merchant, one should not be protected against being cheated?**

The Gemara explains that an ordinary merchant is protected against being cheated. **Rav Nachman said in the name of Rav: Rabbi Judah's teaching applies to a merchant who is a broker. What is the reason? A broker surely knows how much the goods are worth, and, if in agreeing to be underpaid, waives any claim against the buyer and sells at a reduced price because the broker has come upon other goods for which the money is needed. Rabbi Judah's** teaching means that the merchant who later wishes to retract from the sale that involved underpayment may not do so.

Rav Nachman's understanding of Rabbi Judah's statement was to the disadvantage of the seller. The Gemara follows with a different explanation of Rabbi Judah's opinion, this one to the advantage of the seller. **Rav Ashi said: What does it mean, THE LAW AGAINST CHEATING DOES NOT APPLY TO A MERCHANT WHO IS UNDERPAID? It means that a merchant is not subject to the normal one-sixth rule defining cheating, that is, the seller may retract a sale even if underpaid by less than one-sixth.**

Apparently, the Gemara does not accept Rav Ashi's explanation of Rabbi Judah's statement, for it concludes the discussion by pointing to a *baraita* that supports Rav Nachman's explanation of Rabbi Judah's opinion: **A *baraita* was taught supporting the position of Rav Nachman: RABBI JUDAH SAYS: THE LAW AGAINST CHEATING DOES NOT PROTECT A MERCHANT, FOR A MERCHANT IS AN EXPERT.** The merchant knows well the correct value of the items for sale, and in Rabbi Judah's view, does not need the protection of the law provided by the Rabbis.

Rav Ashi was a leading Sage of the fourth and fifth centuries. Traditionally, he was credited with being the editor of the Babylonian Talmud; however, most scholars today believe that, although he may have organized and preserved much valuable material from previous generations, the Talmud was not redacted until after his time. He headed the Sura academy for over half a century and is considered one of the major rabbinic authorities as the amoraic period drew to a close.

What's Your Opinion?

Should a merchant be protected against being underpaid? Should we assume that a merchant knows the merchandise and, if selling it for less, has reason to do so? Should a merchant who undercharged a customer, not realizing this fact until afterward, be allowed to rescind the sale?

Consider This Case

In 1990, a case involving thirteen-year-old Brian Wrzesinski gained national attention. Brian, an avid baseball card collector, saw a 1968 Nolan Ryan/Jerry Koosman rookie baseball card at the Ball-Mart in Itasca, Illinois. The label on the card read $1,200, but it looked a little like $12.00. The clerk was new and inexperienced and sold the card to Brian for $12.00.

Later in the day, Joe Irmen, the owner of Ball-Mart, returned to the store and learned what had happened. He was upset and angry. He called Brian and asked him to return the card. Brian refused, saying that with baseball cards, it was customary to bargain for the best deal possible. He said that it was not his fault if the clerk was incompetent. Irmen said that Brian knew the worth of the card and was aware that the clerk had misread the label.

The case went to court. Do you think that Brian should have returned the card and taken back his $12.00? How do you think the judge should have ruled?

R E V I E W I N G   T H E   T E X T

Bava Metzia 49b

Mishnah: **AN OVERCHARGE OR AN UNDERPAYMENT OF FOUR SILVER PIECES ON AN ITEM WORTH TWENTY-FOUR SILVER PIECES, WHICH MAKE A *SELA,* THAT IS, ONE-SIXTH OF THE PURCHASE PRICE, IS CONSIDERED CHEATING.**

AFTER BEING OVERCHARGED, HOW LONG DOES A BUYER HAVE TO RETRACT? AS LONG AS IT TAKES TO SHOW THE ARTICLE TO A MERCHANT OR TO A RELATIVE.

RABBI TARFON TAUGHT IN LYDDA: AN OVERCHARGE OR AN UNDERPAYMENT OF EIGHT SILVER PIECES ON AN ITEM WORTH A *SELA,* THAT IS, ONE-THIRD OF THE PURCHASE PRICE, IS CONSIDERED CHEATING.

SO THE MERCHANTS OF LYDDA REJOICED.

HE SAID TO THEM: A BUYER HAS ALL DAY LONG TO RETRACT.

THEY SAID TO HIM: LET RABBI TARFON LEAVE US AS WE WERE. AND THEY REVERTED TO FOLLOW THE RULING OF THE SAGES.

Bava Metzia 50b

Gemara: **Rava said: The law is: If there is an overcharge of less than one-sixth, the sale is valid; if it is more than one-sixth, the sale is canceled; if it is exactly one-sixth, the sale is valid, but the seller must refund the overcharge. And in both of the latter two cases, the buyer's time to retract is as long as it takes to show the article to a merchant or to a relative.**

Bava Metzia 50b–51a

Mishnah: **AFTER BEING OVERCHARGED, HOW LONG DOES A BUYER HAVE TO RETRACT? AS LONG AS IT TAKES TO SHOW THE ARTICLE TO A MERCHANT OR TO A RELATIVE.**

Gemara: **Rav Nachman said: This Mishnah, restricting the time in which one may retract, applies only to a buyer who was overcharged. However, a seller who was underpaid may always retract.**

Shall we say that the Mishnah supports the view of Rav Nachman? For the Mishnah says: THE MERCHANTS OF LYDDA REVERTED TO FOLLOW THE RULING OF THE SAGES. Now this is understandable if you say that a seller may always retract, for then Rabbi Tarfon's ruling, increasing the time available for retracting, applied only to buyers, and the merchants reverted to follow the ruling of the Sages to avoid giving buyers any additional time. But if you were to say that Rabbi Tarfon's ruling, increasing the time limit, applied to the seller as well as to the buyer, then what difference would it make to the merchants, for the enactment benefiting the buyer would also benefit the seller?

The merchants of Lydda do not often make the mistake of receiving an underpayment.

The landlord of Rami bar Chama sold some wine but made a mistake, undercharging the buyer. Rami found him to be sad and said to him, "Why are you sad?"

He said to him, "I sold some wine and made a mistake."

Rami said to him, "Go and retract."

His landlord replied, "I have delayed longer than the time necessary to show it to a merchant or a relative."

Rami sent him to Rav Nachman, who said to him, "The Mishnah restricting the time in which one may retract applies only to a buyer who was overcharged. However, a seller who was underpaid may always retract."

What is the reason for Rav Nachman's ruling that restricts the time allowed to a buyer to retract from a sale but allows a seller an unlimited amount of time?

The buyer, who has the purchase in hand, goes around and shows it, and people say whether or not the purchase was a mistake. On the other hand, the seller, who does not have the purchase in hand, must wait until coming upon an item like the one sold, and only then can know whether or not the sale was a mistake.

Bava Metzia 51a

Mishnah: **THE LAW AGAINST CHEATING APPLIES BOTH TO A BUYER WHO IS OVERCHARGED AND TO A SELLER WHO IS UNDERPAID.**

JUST AS THE LAW AGAINST CHEATING APPLIES TO AN ORDINARY PERSON WHO IS OVERCHARGED, SO IT APPLIES TO A MERCHANT WHO IS UNDERPAID.

RABBI JUDAH SAYS: THE LAW AGAINST CHEATING DOES NOT APPLY TO A MERCHANT WHO IS UNDERPAID.

WHOEVER IS CHEATED HAS THE ADVANTAGE: A BUYER WHO IS CHEATED MAY SAY EITHER: GIVE ME BACK MY MONEY, OR GIVE ME BACK THE AMOUNT BY WHICH YOU CHEATED ME.

Mishnah: **RABBI JUDAH SAYS: THE LAW AGAINST CHEATING DOES NOT APPLY TO A MERCHANT WHO IS UNDERPAID.**

Gemara: **Is it right that by virtue of being a merchant, one should not be protected against being cheated?**

Rav Nachman said in the name of Rav: Rabbi Judah's teaching applies to a merchant who is a broker. What is the reason? A broker surely knows how much the goods are worth, and, if in agreeing to be underpaid, waives any claim against the buyer and sells at a reduced price because the broker has come upon other goods for which the money is needed. Rabbi Judah's teaching means that the merchant who later wishes to retract from the sale that involved underpayment may not do so.

Rav Ashi said: What does it mean, THE LAW AGAINST CHEATING DOES NOT APPLY TO A MERCHANT WHO IS UNDERPAID? It means that a merchant is not subject to the normal one-sixth rule defining cheating, that is, the seller may retract a sale even if underpaid by less than one-sixth.

A *baraita* was taught supporting the position of Rav Nachman: RABBI JUDAH SAYS: THE LAW AGAINST CHEATING DOES NOT PROTECT A MERCHANT, FOR A MERCHANT IS AN EXPERT.

Chapter Six

Fraud

Bava Metzia 59b–60a

אֵין מְעָרְבִין פֵּירוֹת בְּפֵירוֹת אֲפִילוּ חֲדָשִׁים בַּחֲדָשִׁים. וְאֵין צָרִיךְ לוֹמַר חֲדָשִׁים בִּישָׁנִים.

בֶּאֱמֶת אָמְרוּ: בַּיַּיִן הִתִּירוּ לְעָרֵב קָשֶׁה בְּרַךְ, מִפְּנֵי שֶׁהוּא מַשְׁבִּיחוֹ.

אֵין מְעָרְבִין שִׁמְרֵי יַיִן בְּיַיִן, אֲבָל נוֹתֵן לוֹ אֶת שְׁמָרָיו.

מִי שֶׁנִּתְעָרֵב מַיִם בְּיֵינוֹ לֹא יִמְכְּרֶנּוּ בַּחֲנוּת, אֶלָּא אִם כֵּן הוֹדִיעוֹ. וְלֹא לַתַּגָּר אַף עַל פִּי שֶׁהוֹדִיעוֹ, שֶׁאֵינוֹ אֶלָּא לְרַמּוֹת בּוֹ. מָקוֹם שֶׁנָּהֲגוּ לְהַטִּיל מַיִם בַּיַּיִן — יַטִּילוּ.

תָּנוּ רַבָּנָן: אֵין צָרִיךְ לוֹמַר חֲדָשׁוֹת מֵאַרְבַּע וִישָׁנוֹת מִשָּׁלֹשׁ דְּאֵין מְעָרְבִין, אֶלָּא אֲפִילוּ חֲדָשׁוֹת מִשָּׁלֹשׁ וִישָׁנוֹת מֵאַרְבַּע — אֵין מְעָרְבִין, מִפְּנֵי שֶׁאָדָם רוֹצֶה לְיַשְׁנָן.

Mishnah: **ONE MAY NOT MIX PRODUCE FROM DIFFERENT SOURCES,** making it difficult for consumers to judge the quality of the produce they are buying **EVEN IF THEY ARE ALL NEW, AND IT GOES WITHOUT SAYING REGARDING NEW WITH OLD.** Old grain was more valuable than new grain; adding new to the old was a form of deception.

ACTUALLY, although it was generally forbidden to mix products of different quality (e.g., new grain with old grain), **THE RABBIS**

54

made an exception and **ALLOWED MIXING OF STRONG WINE WITH WEAK BECAUSE STRONG WINE IMPROVES WEAK WINE.**

ONE MAY NOT MIX WINE SEDIMENT of another wine **WITH WINE** being sold, as it may harm its flavor, **BUT A SELLER MAY GIVE A BUYER THE SEDIMENT OF THE WINE BEING PURCHASED,** and the seller is not required to remove it before selling the wine.

SOMEONE WHOSE WINE WAS MIXED WITH WATER MAY NOT SELL IT IN A STORE WITHOUT INFORMING THE BUYER, NOR MAY IT BE SOLD TO A MERCHANT EVEN IF THE LATTER IS INFORMED, FOR THE MERCHANT WOULD WANT IT FOR NO REASON OTHER THAN TO DECEIVE OTHERS. IN A PLACE WHERE IT IS THE CUSTOM TO DILUTE THE WINE WITH WATER, ONE MAY DILUTE IT.

Gemara: **The Rabbis have taught in a *baraita*: IT GOES WITHOUT SAYING THAT IF THE NEW GRAIN WAS SELLING AT FOUR *SEAH*S PER *SELA* AND THE OLD GRAIN AT** the higher price of **THREE, A SELLER MAY NOT MIX THE NEW WITH THE OLD. BUT EVEN IF** a select supply of **THE NEW GRAIN WAS SELLING AT THREE *SEAH*S PER *SELA* AND THE OLD GRAIN AT** the lower price of **FOUR, THE SELLER STILL MAY NOT MIX THE MORE EXPENSIVE NEW GRAIN INTO THE OLD BECAUSE THE BUYER MAY WANT TO AGE THE GRAIN.**

Bava Metzia 60a

אָמַר רַב נַחְמָן: וּבֵין הַגִּיתוֹת שָׁנוּ.

וְהָאִידָנָא דְּקָא מְעַרְבִי שֶׁלֹּא בֵּין הַגִּתּוֹת.

אָמַר רַב פַּפָּא: דְּיָדְעִי וְקָא מָחֲלִי.

רַב אַחָא בְּרֵיהּ דְּרַב אִיקָא אָמַר: הָא מַנִּי?

רַבִּי אַחָא הִיא. דְּתַנְיָא: רַבִּי אַחָא מַתִּיר בְּדָבָר הַנִּטְעַם.

Gemara: **Rav Nachman said: Mixing strong wine with weak wine is allowed only while the wine is still in the wine presses** in the early stages of production, before each type of wine has acquired its distinctive flavor.

Rav Pappa was a leading rabbinic authority in the fourth century. He was a student of Rava and Abaye and a teacher of Rav Ashi. He acquired wealth trading poppy seeds and brewing date beer. His opinions are frequently quoted in the Babylonian Talmud, often as authoritative. He headed a famous academy near Sura for nineteen years until his death.

Rabbi Acha lived near the end of the tannaitic period. His teachings appear in *baraitot* but not in the Mishnah.

Rav Acha the son of Rav Ika was a fourth-century *Amora*.

In light of Rav Nachman's restriction, the Gemara raises a question: **But nowadays they mix strong wine with weak wine even after it has been taken from the presses.**

The Gemara provides two answers to this difficulty: **Rav Pappa said: It is allowed because people know about it and accept it.**

Rav Acha the son of Rav Ika said: Whose view is followed in this case? It is that of Rabbi Acha, for it was taught in a *baraita:* RABBI ACHA PERMITS MIXING OF STRONG WINE WITH WEAK WINE WHERE THE CUSTOMER IS ABLE TO TASTE THE WINE BEFORE BUYING IT.

What's Your Opinion?

Do you think it is right to forbid mixing of different kinds of grains even when the grain that is mixed in is worth more than the other grain?

Do you think that the opinions of Rav Pappa and Rabbi Acha are adequate explanations to allow for the mixing of wine?

Do you think that the Mishnah is too harsh in ruling that one may never sell diluted wine to a merchant?

Consider This Case

Fred had a collection of ancient coins, which he had accumulated over a period of many years. Eventually he lost interest in coin collecting and decided to sell his collection. Among his coins were about a half-dozen replicas. These were coins made to look like ancient coins but were actually made quite recently. Replicas were often sold as authentic antiquities. They had only limited value as replicas.

Should Fred include the replicas in his sale (making clear that they are replicas) if he sells his collection to a private collector? If he sells to a coin dealer?

לֹא יָבוֹר אֶת הַגְּרִיסִין, דִּבְרֵי אַבָּא שָׁאוּל.

וַחֲכָמִים מַתִּירִין. וּמוֹדִים שֶׁלֹּא יָבוֹר מֵעַל פִּי מְגוּרָה, שֶׁאֵינוֹ אֶלָּא כְּגוֹנֵב אֶת הָעַיִן.

אֵין מְפַרְכְּסִין לֹא אֶת הָאָדָם וְלֹא אֶת הַבְּהֵמָה וְלֹא אֶת הַכֵּלִים.

Mishnah: A SELLER MAY NOT SIFT CRUSHED BEANS TO REMOVE THE REFUSE, for this leads to increasing their price more than their improved appearance merits. **THESE ARE THE WORDS OF ABBA SAUL.**

BUT THE SAGES ALLOW IT. HOWEVER, THEY AGREE THAT THE SELLER MAY NOT SIFT JUST AT THE OPENING OF THE BIN, FOR THIS WOULD SIMPLY BE DECEPTION.

ONE MAY NOT PAINT and thereby hide the true appearance of **A PERSON OR AN ANIMAL OR UTENSILS.**

Abba Saul was a second-century *Tanna,* a younger contemporary of Rabbi Akiva. His views, which are frequently cited as minority opinions in the Mishnah, often influenced the legal decisions of later generations.

Bava Metzia 60b

מַאן חֲכָמִים? רַבִּי אַחָא, דְּתַנְיָא: רַבִּי אַחָא מַתִּיר בְּדָבָר הַנִּרְאֶה.

Gemara: Who are the Sages who permit the sifting of beans? It was Rabbi Acha, for it was taught in a *baraita:* **RABBI ACHA PERMITS MERCHANDISE TO BE ALTERED IF THE ALTERATION IS VISIBLE TO THE CUSTOMER.**

Bava Metzia 60b

תָּנוּ רַבָּנָן: אֵין מְשַׁרְבְּטִין אֶת הַבְּהֵמָה, וְאֵין נוֹפְחִין בַּקְּרָבַיִים, וְאֵין שׁוֹרִין אֶת הַבָּשָׂר בְּמַיִם.

מַאי "אֵין מְשַׁרְבְּטִין"? הָכָא תַּרְגִּמוּ: מַיָּא דְחִיזְרָא, זְעֵירֵי אֲמַר רַב כָּהֲנָא: מִזְקַפְתָּא.

שְׁמוּאֵל שָׁרָא לְמִרְמָא תּוּמֵי לְסַרְבְּלָא. רַב יְהוּדָה שָׁרָא לְכַסְכּוּסֵי קַרְמֵי. רַבָּה שָׁרָא לְמֵידַק צָרְדֵי. רָבָא שָׁרָא לְצַלּוֹמֵי גִּירֵי. רַב פַּפָּא בַּר שְׁמוּאֵל שָׁרָא לְצַלּוֹמֵי דִיקוּלֵי.

Ze'iri lived in the third century. He was born in Babylonia but studied with Rabbi Yochanan in Palestine. He later returned to Babylonia, where he transmitted Palestinian traditions.

When the Gemara speaks of Rav Judah, it refers to Rav Judah bar Ezekiel, a student of Rav and Samuel and a leading Sage of the third century. He and his older colleague, Rav Huna, are frequently cited as disputants in the Babylonian Talmud. When the academy in Nehardea was destroyed in 259 C.E., Rav Judah founded an academy in Pumbedita, which he led for the next forty years. The academy at Pumbedita remained a center for Jewish learning for some eight centuries.

Rabbah, cited in the Talmud without his father's name, refers to Rabbah bar Nachmani, a student of both Rav Huna and Rav Judah who lived during the third and fourth centuries. A few years after the death of Rav Judah, Rabbah assumed the leadership of the academy in Pumbedita, a position he held for over twenty years. The academy flourished under his leadership, attracting many outstanding students. The Talmud records many disputes between him and his colleague, Rav Joseph. In almost every instance, the law follows Rabbah.

Rav Pappa bar Samuel was a rabbinic Sage who lived during the third and fourth centuries. He made his home in Pumbedita.

וְהָא אֲנַן תְּנַן: אֵין מְפַרְכְּסִין לֹא אֶת הָאָדָם וְלֹא אֶת הַבְּהֵמָה וְלֹא אֶת הַכֵּלִים!

לָא קַשְׁיָא, הָא — בַּחֲדַתֵּי, הָא — בַּעֲתִיקֵי.

Gemara: **Our Rabbis taught in a *baraita*: ONE MAY NOT STIFFEN AN ANIMAL'S HAIR, NOR MAY ONE ENLARGE AN ANIMAL'S INTESTINES, NOR MAY ONE SOAK MEAT IN WATER.**

These were ways of making an animal or meat appear larger than they were.

The Gemara inquires: **What does it mean, ONE MAY NOT STIFFEN AN ANIMAL'S HAIR? Here they explained it as giving the animal bran broth to drink. Ze'iri said in the name of Rav Kahana: It was done by brushing the animal's hair.**

The Gemara then describes several practices for improving the appearance of goods that the Rabbis allowed: **Samuel permitted putting fringes on a coat. Rav Judah permitted polishing fine clothes. Rabbah permitted beating rough cloth. Rava permitted painting arrows. Rav Pappa bar Samuel permitted painting baskets.**

The Gemara questions these practices: **But have we not learned in the Mishnah: ONE MAY NOT PAINT A PERSON OR AN ANIMAL OR UTENSILS?** Thus none of these practices should be allowed.

There is no contradiction. The practices permitted by the Rabbis refer to new articles. The prohibition in the Mishnah refers to old ones.

Consider These Cases

Deborah had cracks on the brickwork in the front of her house. Before selling it, she had the bricks covered with aluminum siding. Was this an acceptable action?

Dan had an auto accident involving the front end of his car. He had everything repaired; not a scratch was visible. He then put his car up for sale. When potential buyers asked about accidents, he responded honestly, but if he wasn't asked, he didn't volunteer any information. Did he do the right thing?

Bava Metzia 59b–60a

Mishnah: **ONE MAY NOT MIX PRODUCE FROM DIFFERENT SOURCES EVEN IF THEY ARE ALL NEW, AND IT GOES WITHOUT SAYING REGARDING NEW WITH OLD.**

ACTUALLY, THE RABBIS ALLOWED MIXING OF STRONG WINE WITH WEAK BECAUSE STRONG WINE IMPROVES WEAK WINE.

ONE MAY NOT MIX WINE SEDIMENT WITH WINE, BUT A SELLER MAY GIVE A BUYER THE SEDIMENT OF THE WINE BEING PURCHASED.

SOMEONE WHOSE WINE WAS MIXED WITH WATER MAY NOT SELL IT IN A STORE WITHOUT INFORMING THE BUYER, NOR MAY IT BE SOLD TO A MERCHANT EVEN IF THE LATTER IS INFORMED, FOR THE MERCHANT WOULD WANT IT FOR NO REASON OTHER THAN TO DECEIVE OTHERS. IN A PLACE WHERE IT IS THE CUSTOM TO DILUTE THE WINE WITH WATER, ONE MAY DILUTE IT.

Gemara: **The Rabbis have taught in a *baraita*:** IT GOES WITHOUT SAYING THAT IF THE NEW GRAIN WAS SELLING AT FOUR *SEAH*S PER *SELA* AND THE OLD GRAIN AT THREE, A SELLER MAY NOT MIX THE NEW WITH THE OLD. BUT EVEN IF THE NEW GRAIN WAS SELLING AT THREE *SEAH*S PER *SELA* AND THE OLD GRAIN AT FOUR, THE SELLER STILL MAY NOT MIX THE MORE EXPENSIVE NEW GRAIN WITH THE OLD BECAUSE THE BUYER MAY WISH TO AGE THE GRAIN.

Bava Metzia 60a

Gemara: **Rav Nachman said: Mixing strong wine with weak wine is allowed only while the wine is still in the wine presses.**

But nowadays they mix strong wine with weak wine even after it has been taken from the presses.

Rav Pappa said: It is allowed because people know about it and accept it.

Rav Acha the son of Rav Ika said: Whose view is followed in this case? It is that of Rabbi Acha, for it was taught in a *baraita:* RABBI ACHA PERMITS MIXING OF STRONG WINE WITH WEAK WINE WHERE THE CUSTOMER IS ABLE TO TASTE THE WINE BEFORE BUYING IT.

Bava Metzia 60a

Mishnah: **A SELLER MAY NOT SIFT CRUSHED BEANS TO REMOVE THE REFUSE. THESE ARE THE WORDS OF ABBA SAUL.**

BUT THE SAGES ALLOW IT. HOWEVER, THEY AGREE THAT THE SELLER MAY NOT SIFT JUST AT THE OPENING OF THE BIN, FOR THIS WOULD SIMPLY BE DECEPTION.

ONE MAY NOT PAINT A PERSON OR AN ANIMAL OR UTENSILS.

Bava Metzia 60b

Gemara: **Who are the Sages who permit the sifting of beans? It was Rabbi Acha, for it was taught in a *baraita:* RABBI ACHA PERMITS MERCHANDISE TO BE ALTERED IF THE ALTERATION IS VISIBLE TO THE CUSTOMER.**

Bava Metzia 60b

Gemara: **Our Rabbis taught in a *baraita:* ONE MAY NOT STIFFEN AN ANIMAL'S HAIR, NOR MAY ONE ENLARGE AN ANIMAL'S INTESTINES, NOR MAY ONE SOAK MEAT IN WATER.**

What does it mean, ONE MAY NOT STIFFEN AN ANIMAL'S HAIR? Here they explained it as giving the animal bran broth to drink. Ze'iri said in the name of Rav Kahana: It was done by brushing the animal's hair.

Samuel permitted putting fringes on a coat. Rav Judah permitted polishing fine clothes. Rabbah permitted beating rough cloth. Rava permitted painting arrows. Rav Pappa bar Samuel permitted painting baskets.

But have we not learned in the Mishnah: ONE MAY NOT PAINT A PERSON OR AN ANIMAL OR UTENSILS?

There is no contradiction. The practices permitted by the Rabbis refer to new articles. The prohibition in the Mishnah refers to old ones.

Chapter Seven

Competition

Bava Metzia 60a

רַבִּי יְהוּדָה אוֹמֵר: לֹא יְחַלֵּק הַחֶנְוָנִי קְלָיוֹת וֶאֱגוֹזִין לַתִּינוֹקוֹת, מִפְּנֵי שֶׁהוּא מַרְגִּילָן לָבֹא אֶצְלוֹ. וַחֲכָמִים מַתִּירִין.

וְלֹא יִפְחוֹת אֶת הַשַּׁעַר, וַחֲכָמִים אוֹמְרִים: זָכוּר לַטּוֹב.

Mishnah: **RABBI JUDAH SAID: A STOREKEEPER MAY NOT DISTRIBUTE PARCHED GRAIN OR NUTS TO CHILDREN IN ORDER TO ENCOURAGE THEM TO SHOP IN THAT STORE, BUT THE SAGES PERMIT IT.**

FURTHERMORE, RABBI JUDAH SAID: A STOREKEEPER MAY NOT SELL GOODS AT LESS THAN THE MARKET PRICE, BUT THE SAGES SAY: ONE WHO DOES SO IS REMEMBERED FOR GOOD.

Bava Metzia 60a

מַאי טַעְמַיְיהוּ דְּרַבָּנַן? — דְּאָמַר לֵיהּ: אֲנָא מְפַלֵּיגְנָא אַמְגוּזֵי, וְאַתְּ פְּלֵיג שִׁסְקֵי.

"וְלֹא יִפְחוֹת אֶת הַשַּׁעַר וַחֲכָמִים אוֹמְרִים: זָכוּר לַטּוֹב וְכוּ'".
מַאי טַעְמָא דְּרַבָּנַן? מִשּׁוּם דְּקָא מַרְוַח לְתַרְעָא.

Gemara: **What is the reason that the Sages allow a storekeeper to distribute treats to children? Because the storekeeper can reply: I am distributing nuts, and you may distribute plums.**

RABBI JUDAH SAID: A STOREKEEPER MAY NOT SELL GOODS AT LESS THAN THE MARKET PRICE, BUT THE SAGES SAY: ONE WHO DOES SO IS REMEMBERED FOR GOOD. What is the reason that the Sages allow this practice? Because one who sells for less helps to reduce the market price.

What's Your Opinion?

Do you agree with Rabbi Judah or with the Sages? Should a merchant be allowed to offer incentives to buy his products? Should there be restrictions on these incentives? If so, what kinds? Are there circumstances when it would be wrong for a storekeeper to lower his prices below market levels?

Consider This Case

In a small midwestern town, there are three service stations. Tom and Dick are partners and own one of the stations. Harry owns another service station, and Jack the third one. The three stations compete for a limited number of customers. Tom proposes to Dick that they build their customer base by reducing the price of their gas by fifteen cents a gallon. He says that they can survive for a long time on a profit margin of only a penny or two per gallon. He believes that if they can bring customers into their station with the low-priced gas, the customers will stick with them even if they eventually raise the price.

Dick objects to this idea. He points out that although the two of them can afford to make little or no money for a period of time, Harry and Jack would not be able to do so. Dick believes that if he and Tom were to follow Tom's suggestion, they would probably drive Harry and Jack out of business altogether. It might be good for their business, but in Dick's view, it would not be the right thing to do.

Do you agree with Tom or with Dick?

אָמַר רַב הוּנָא: הַאי בַּר מְבוֹאָה דְּאוֹקֵי רֵיחַיָּא, וְאָתָא בַּר מְבוֹאָה חַבְרֵיהּ וְקָמוֹקֵי גַּבֵּיהּ — דִּינָא הוּא דִּמְעַכֵּב עִילָוֵיהּ, דְּאָמַר לֵיהּ: קָא פָּסְקַתְּ לֵיהּ לְחַיּוּתִי.

Gemara: Rav Huna said: If the resident of an alley has set up a mill, and then another resident of the alley wants to set one up next door, the law is that the first one may prevent it, by making the claim, "You are obstructing my livelihood."

אָמַר לֵיהּ רָבִינָא לְרָבָא: לֵימָא, רַב הוּנָא דְּאָמַר כְּרַבִּי יְהוּדָה? דִּתְנַן, רַבִּי יְהוּדָה אוֹמֵר: לֹא יְחַלֵּק חֶנְוָנִי קְלָיוֹת וֶאֱגוֹזִין לַתִּינוֹקוֹת, מִפְּנֵי שֶׁמַּרְגִּילָן אֶצְלוֹ, וַחֲכָמִים מַתִּירִין.

אֲפִילוּ תֵּימָא רַבָּנַן, עַד כָּאן לָא פְּלִיגִי רַבָּנַן עֲלֵיהּ דְּרַבִּי יְהוּדָה הָתָם — אֶלָּא דְּאָמַר לֵיהּ: אֲנָא קָמְפַלְגִינָא אַמְגוּזֵי, אַתְּ פְּלוֹג שִׁיּוּסְקֵי.

אֲבָל הָכָא אֲפִילוּ רַבָּנַן מוֹדוּ, דְּאָמַר לֵיהּ: קָא פָּסְקַתְּ לֵיהּ לְחַיּוּתִי.

מֵיתִיבֵי: עוֹשֶׂה אָדָם חֲנוּת בְּצַד חֲנוּתוֹ שֶׁל חֲבֵירוֹ, וּמֶרְחָץ בְּצַד מֶרְחָצוֹ שֶׁל חֲבֵירוֹ, וְאֵינוֹ יָכוֹל לִמְחוֹת בְּיָדוֹ, מִפְּנֵי שֶׁיָּכוֹל לוֹמַר לוֹ: אַתָּה עוֹשֶׂה בְּתוֹךְ שֶׁלְּךָ וַאֲנִי עוֹשֶׂה בְּתוֹךְ שֶׁלִּי!

תַּנָּאֵי הִיא; דְּתַנְיָא: כּוֹפִין בְּנֵי מְבוֹאוֹת זֶה אֶת זֶה שֶׁלֹּא לְהוֹשִׁיב בֵּינֵיהֶן לֹא חַיָּיט וְלֹא בּוּרְסְקִי, וְלֹא מְלַמֵּד תִּינוֹקוֹת, וְלֹא אֶחָד מִבְּנֵי בַּעֲלֵי אוּמָּנִיּוֹת, וְלִשְׁכֵנוֹ אֵינוֹ כּוֹפֵיהוּ.

רַבָּן שִׁמְעוֹן בֶּן גַּמְלִיאֵל אוֹמֵר: אַף לִשְׁכֵנוֹ כּוֹפֵיהוּ.

אָמַר רַב הוּנָא בְּרֵיהּ דְּרַב יְהוֹשֻׁעַ: פְּשִׁיטָא לִי, בַּר מָתָא אַבַּר מָתָא אַחֲרִיתִי מָצֵי מְעַכֵּב, וְאִי שַׁיָּיךְ בְּכַרְגָּא דְּהָכָא — לָא מָצֵי מְעַכֵּב.

בַּר מְבוֹאָה אַבַּר מְבוֹאָה דְּנַפְשֵׁיהּ — לָא מָצֵי מְעַכֵּב.

בָּעֵי רַב הוּנָא בְּרֵיהּ דְּרַב יְהוֹשֻׁעַ: בַּר מְבוֹאָה אַבַּר מְבוֹאָה אַחֲרִינָא, מַאי? תֵּיקוּ.

אָמַר רַב יוֹסֵף: וּמוֹדֵי רַב הוּנָא בְּמַקְרֵי דַּרְדְּקֵי דְּלָא מָצֵי מְעַכֵּב, דְּאָמַר מָר: קִנְאַת סוֹפְרִים תַּרְבֶּה חָכְמָה.

אָמַר רַב נַחְמָן בַּר יִצְחָק: וּמוֹדֶה רַב הוּנָא בְּרֵיהּ דְּרַב יְהוֹשֻׁעַ בְּרוֹכְלִין הַמַּחֲזִירִין בָּעֲיָירוֹת דְּלָא מָצֵי מְעַכֵּב, דְּאָמַר מָר: עֶזְרָא תִּקֵּן לָהֶן לְיִשְׂרָאֵל שֶׁיִּהְיוּ רוֹכְלִין מַחֲזִירִין בָּעֲיָירוֹת, כְּדֵי שֶׁיִּהְיוּ תַּכְשִׁיטִין מְצוּיִּין לִבְנוֹת יִשְׂרָאֵל.

וְהָנֵי מִילֵי לְאַהֲדוּרֵי, אֲבָל לְאַקְבּוּעֵי — לָא.

וְאִי צוּרְבָא מֵרַבָּנָן הוּא — אֲפִילּוּ לְאַקְבּוּעֵי נַמִי, כִּי הָא דְּרָבָא שְׁרָא לְהוּ לְרַבִּי יֹאשִׁיָה וּלְרַב עוֹבַדְיָה לְאַקְבּוּעֵי, דְּלָא כְּהִלְכְתָא, מַאי טַעֲמָא? כֵּיוָן דְּרַבָּנָן נִינְהוּ, אָתוּ לְטַרְדוּ מִגִּירְסַיְיהוּ.

Ravina, a student of Rava, was a Sage of the fourth and fifth centuries. Although it is known that the Talmud was not completed until the end of the fifth century or later, Ravina is credited with working in association with Rav Ashi to preserve and edit the talmudic material.

Ravina said to Rava: Shall we say that Rav Huna follows the teaching of Rabbi Judah? For we have learned in a Mishnah: RABBI JUDAH SAYS: A STOREKEEPER MAY NOT DISTRIBUTE PARCHED GRAIN OR NUTS TO CHILDREN IN ORDER TO ENCOURAGE THEM TO SHOP IN THAT STORE, BUT THE SAGES PERMIT IT. It would seem that both Rav Huna and Rabbi Judah follow the same principle: One merchant may not take away customers from another.

The Gemara replies that it is not necessarily so that Rav Huna is in accord with the view of Rabbi Judah. In fact: **You can say that he is in agreement with the Rabbis. For the Rabbis' dispute with Rabbi Judah is on the grounds that one storekeeper can say to another: "I am distributing nuts, and you may distribute plums."**

That is, where two *established* stores exist, the Rabbis believe that each storekeeper may engage in efforts to attract customers. **But here,** where one merchant has an established store and the other wishes to open a new one, **even the Rabbis might**

agree that one merchant may prevent the other from opening up on the grounds **that the former may say, "You are obstructing my livelihood."**

An objection was raised to Rav Huna's ruling from the following *baraita:* A PERSON MAY OPEN A STORE NEXT TO ANOTHER'S STORE OR A BATHHOUSE NEXT TO ANOTHER'S BATHHOUSE, AND THE ESTABLISHED BUSINESS OWNER CANNOT PREVENT IT, BECAUSE THE NEW ONE CAN SAY TO THE ESTABLISHED ONE, "YOU MAY DO AS YOU WISH ON YOUR PROPERTY, AND I MAY DO AS I WISH ON MINE." This *baraita* clearly contradicts Rav Huna's ruling.

The Gemara responds by providing another *baraita,* which includes the view of a *Tanna* who agrees with Rav Huna: **On this matter there is a difference of opinion between** *Tannaim,* **for it was taught in the following** *baraita:* THE RESIDENTS OF AN ALLEY CAN PREVENT ONE ANOTHER FROM BRINGING INTO THEIR ALLEY A TAILOR, A TANNER, A TEACHER, OR OTHER KINDS OF CRAFTSPERSONS, BUT THEY CANNOT PREVENT ONE ANOTHER FROM OPENING UP COMPETING BUSINESSES.

RABBAN SIMEON BEN GAMALIEL SAYS: THEY CAN EVEN PREVENT ONE ANOTHER FROM OPENING COMPETING BUSINESSES. The anonymous opinion in this *baraita,* like the previous *baraita,* contradicts Rav Huna's ruling. However, this *baraita* includes the opinion of Rabban Simeon ben Gamaliel, which provides support for Rav Huna's ruling.

A summary of the rules on setting up competing businesses is now offered: **Rav Huna the son of Rav Joshua said: It is obvious to me that a resident of one town can prevent the resident of another town from coming in and setting up a competing business. However, one who pays taxes in that town may not be prevented.**

The resident of an alley is not able to prevent another resident of the same alley from setting up a competing business. The Gemara had previously pointed to a dispute among *Tannaim.* An anonymous *Tanna* had said, "They cannot prevent one another from opening up competing businesses," whereas Rabban Simeon ben Gamaliel said that they could prevent one another from setting up competing businesses. Rav Huna had

Rav Huna the son of Rav Joshua lived during the second half of the fourth century and the very beginning of the fifth. He was a student of Rava and Abaye and a close friend and business partner of Rav Pappa.

From time to time, the Gemara admits that it has no answer to a particular problem by stating תיקו, "the question stands." The traditional interpretation of the word תיקו is that it is an acronym for תשבי יתרץ קושיות ואיבעיות, "The Tishbite [Elijah the Prophet] will solve all questions and problems."

agreed with Rabban Simeon ben Gamaliel. Now, Rav Huna the son of Rav Joshua agrees with the anonymous *Tanna* and rejects the view of Rabban Simeon ben Gamaliel and Rav Huna.

Rav Huna the son Rav Joshua asked: May the resident of an alley prevent the resident of the another alley in the same town from coming in and setting up a competing business? The question stands.

What's Your Opinion?

Should there be any laws to protect businesses from competition? Is it right to allow a competing business to open next door to an existing one?

Consider This Case

The Green Family Pharmacy has been in the Riverside neighborhood for over fifty years. All agree that Green's pharmacists have served the community with care and competence. Now a representative of a national chain of pharmacies appears before the Riverside City Council asking for permission to open a pharmacy there.

Jacob Green stands before the city council reminding the council members of the extra touches his family has lent in its service to the community for three generations. He reminds them of their pharmacy's policy to be available twenty-four hours a day and of the many times that they opened up in the middle of the night to provide a customer with needed medication. He tells them that if the chain store opens, he is sure that the Green Family Pharmacy will soon close.

If you were a member of the city council, would you vote to allow the chain store to open?

Rav Joseph (bar Chiyya) was a prominent fourth-century Sage. He was appointed head of the academy in Pumbedita but died two and one-half years later. Hundreds of his saying are found throughout the Talmud.

The Gemara now provides an exception to Rav Huna's ruling that someone may not come into an alley and set up a competing business: **Rav Joseph said: Rav Huna agrees that a teacher cannot prevent another teacher from setting up in the same alley, for the master has said, "Jealousy among scholars**

increases wisdom." Although Rav Huna, as a general rule, would prevent alley residents from opening up competing businesses, he makes an exception in the case of teachers, because competition among teachers improves the quality of teaching.

The Gemara offers another exception to the rule: **Rav Nachman bar Isaac said: Rav Huna the son of Rav Joshua agrees that an established merchant cannot prevent peddlers who move about in the towns from coming in and selling their wares, for the master has said that Ezra made an ordinance for Israel that peddlers may move about in the towns so that cosmetics will be available to the daughters of Israel.**

And this exception applies to moving about and selling but not to opening a store.

But a peddler who is a rabbinic scholar may even open a store, just as Rava allowed Rav Josiah and Rav Obadiah to open stores even though it was not according to the law. What is the reason for this exception? It is because they are Rabbis, who would be diverted from their studies if they had to move about and sell.

Rav Nachman bar Isaac was one of the leading rabbinic authorities of the fourth century. After the death of Rava, he became head of the Pumbedita academy.

The Bible relates that Ezra the scribe helped to restore the Torah to its prime place in Israel after the Babylonian exile. According to the Rabbis, he introduced a number of ordinances for the welfare of the people; this was one of them.

Rav Josiah and Rav Obadiah were fourth-century Sages who were students of Rava.

What's Your Opinion

Rav Huna wishes to protect established businesspeople and therefore rules to restrict residents of an alley from opening competing businesses. But even Rav Huna, we learn, makes an exception in the case of teachers because he believes that competition improves the quality of education. ("Jealousy among scholars increases wisdom.") Do you agree with this viewpoint?

In talmudic times, Rabbis were given certain advantages in the market so that they would need to spend less time in their business pursuits and be able to spend more time in their studies. Do you think that this was a good idea?

Rabbis were permitted to open competing stores, a privilege denied to others. They were relieved of certain taxes, and competing merchants in the market were required to delay their sales until the Rabbis finished selling their wares.

Consider This Case

You are a member of the Supreme Court. Lawyers for a group of parents in a midwestern state argue that education suffers in their community because of a lack of competition. Most families cannot afford to send their children to expensive private schools, so they send them to the public school, where the quality of education is poor. They propose that, with government assistance, families be allowed to send their children to the school of their choice, public or private. They say that with competition for students, the quality of education will improve at all of the schools.

Opponents argue that the proposed change would drain funds from the public schools and that these schools would become even weaker than they are now. They point out that the public schools provide costly education for special students, which the private schools do not do. Finally, they say that most private schools have a religious orientation and that public funds should not be used to advance religious teachings.

What position would you take as a member of the Court?

R E V I E W I N G   T H E   T E X T

Bava Metzia 60a

Mishnah: **RABBI JUDAH SAID: A STOREKEEPER MAY NOT DISTRIBUTE PARCHED GRAIN OR NUTS TO CHILDREN IN ORDER TO ENCOURAGE THEM TO SHOP IN THAT STORE, BUT THE SAGES PERMIT IT.**

FURTHERMORE, RABBI JUDAH SAID: A STOREKEEPER MAY NOT SELL GOODS AT LESS THAN THE MARKET PRICE, BUT THE SAGES SAY: ONE WHO DOES SO IS REMEMBERED FOR GOOD.

Bava Metzia 60a

Gemara: **What is the reason that the Sages allow a storekeeper to distribute treats to children? Because the storekeeper can reply: I am distributing nuts, and you may distribute plums.**

RABBI JUDAH SAID: A STOREKEEPER MAY NOT SELL GOODS AT LESS THAN THE MARKET PRICE, BUT THE SAGES SAY: ONE WHO DOES SO IS REMEMBERED FOR GOOD. What is the reason that the Sages allow this practice? Because one who sells for less helps to reduce the market price.

Bava Batra 21b

Gemara: **Rav Huna said: If the resident of an alley has set up a mill, and then another resident of the alley wants to set one up next door, the law is that the first one may prevent it, by making the claim, "You are obstructing my livelihood."**

Bava Batra 21b

Ravina said to Rava: Shall we say that Rav Huna follows the teaching of Rabbi Judah? For we have learned in a Mishnah: RABBI JUDAH SAYS: A STOREKEEPER MAY NOT DISTRIBUTE PARCHED GRAIN OR NUTS TO CHILDREN IN ORDER TO ENCOURAGE THEM TO SHOP IN HIS STORE, BUT THE SAGES PERMIT IT.

You can say that he is in agreement with the Rabbis. For the Rabbis' dispute with Rabbi Judah is on the grounds that one storekeeper can say to another: "I am distributing nuts, and you may distribute plums."

But here, even the Rabbis might agree that the former may say, "You are obstructing my livelihood."

An objection was raised to Rav Huna's ruling from the following *baraita:* A PERSON MAY OPEN A STORE NEXT TO ANOTHER'S STORE OR A BATHHOUSE NEXT TO ANOTHER'S BATHHOUSE, AND THE ESTABLISHED BUSINESS OWNER CANNOT PREVENT IT, BECAUSE THE NEW ONE CAN SAY TO THE ESTABLISHED ONE, "YOU MAY DO AS YOU WISH ON YOUR PROPERTY, AND I MAY DO AS I WISH ON MINE."

On this matter there is a difference of opinion between *Tannaim,* for it was taught in the following *baraita:* THE RESIDENTS OF AN ALLEY CAN PREVENT ONE ANOTHER FROM BRINGING INTO THEIR ALLEY A TAILOR, A TANNER, A TEACHER, OR OTHER KINDS OF CRAFTSPERSONS, BUT THEY CANNOT PREVENT ONE ANOTHER FROM OPENING UP COMPETING BUSINESSES.

RABBAN SIMEON BEN GAMALIEL SAYS: THEY CAN EVEN PREVENT ONE ANOTHER FROM OPENING COMPETING BUSINESSES.

Rav Huna the son of Rav Joshua said: It is obvious to me that a resident of one town can prevent the resident of another town from coming in and setting up a competing business. However, one who pays taxes in that town may not be prevented.

The resident of an alley is not able to prevent another resident of the same alley from setting up a competing business.

Rav Huna the son Rav Joshua asked: May the resident of an alley prevent the resident of the another alley in the same town from coming in and setting up a competing business? The question stands.

Rav Joseph said: Rav Huna agrees that a teacher cannot prevent another teacher from setting up in the same alley, for the master has said, "Jealousy among scholars increases wisdom."

Rav Nachman bar Isaac said: Rav Huna the son of Rav Joshua agrees that an established merchant cannot prevent peddlers who move about in the towns from coming in and selling their wares, for the master has said that Ezra made an ordinance for Israel that peddlers may move about in the towns so that cosmetics will be available to the daughters of Israel.

And this exception applies to moving about and selling but not to opening a store.

But a peddler who is a rabbinic scholar may even open a store, just as Rava allowed Rav Josiah and Rav Obadiah to open stores even though it was not according to the law. What is the reason for this exception? It is because they are Rabbis, who would be diverted from their studies if they had to move about and sell.

Chapter Eight

Scales and Measures

Bava Batra 88a–b

הַסִּיטוֹן מְקַנֵּחַ מִדּוֹתָיו אֶחָד לִשְׁלֹשִׁים יוֹם, וּבַעַל הַבַּיִת —
אֶחָד לִשְׁנֵים עָשָׂר חֹדֶשׁ.

רַבָּן שִׁמְעוֹן בֶּן גַּמְלִיאֵל אוֹמֵר: חִלּוּף הַדְּבָרִים.

חֶנְוָנִי מְקַנֵּחַ מִדּוֹתָיו פַּעֲמַיִם בְּשַׁבָּת, וּמְמַחֶה מִשְׁקְלוֹתָיו
פַּעַם אַחַת בְּשַׁבָּת, וּמְקַנֵּחַ מֹאזְנַיִם עַל כָּל מִשְׁקָל וּמִשְׁקָל.

אָמַר רַבָּן שִׁמְעוֹן בֶּן גַּמְלִיאֵל: בַּמֶּה דְבָרִים אֲמוּרִים? בְּלַח,
אֲבָל בְּיָבֵשׁ — אֵינוֹ צָרִיךְ.

וְחַיָּיב לְהַכְרִיעַ לוֹ טֶפַח. הָיָה שׁוֹקֵל לוֹ עַיִן בְּעַיִן — נוֹתֵן לוֹ
גֵּירוּמִין, אֶחָד לַעֲשָׂרָה בְּלַח, וְאֶחָד לְעֶשְׂרִים בְּיָבֵשׁ.

מָקוֹם שֶׁנָּהֲגוּ לָמוֹד בְּדַקָּה — לֹא יָמוֹד בְּגַסָּה, בְּגַסָּה — לֹא
יָמוֹד בְּדַקָּה.

לִמְחוֹק — לֹא יִגְדּוֹשׁ, לִגְדּוֹשׁ — לֹא יִמְחוֹק.

Mishnah: **WHOLESALERS MUST CLEAN THEIR MEASURES
ONCE IN THIRTY DAYS AND HOUSEHOLDERS ONCE EVERY
TWELVE MONTHS.**

**RABBAN SIMEON BEN GAMALIEL SAID: THIS STATEMENT
SHOULD BE REVERSED.**

71

STOREKEEPERS MUST CLEAN THEIR MEASURES TWICE A WEEK, WIPE THEIR WEIGHTS ONCE A WEEK, AND WIPE THEIR SCALES FOR EVERY SINGLE WEIGHING.

RABBAN SIMEON BEN GAMALIEL SAID: WHEN DO THESE RULES APPLY? WHEN LIQUIDS ARE SOLD, BUT FOR DRY PRODUCTS, IT IS NOT NECESSARY.

A STOREKEEPER MUST ALLOW THE SIDE OF THE SCALE WITH THE GOODS TO SINK A HANDBREADTH LOWER THAN THE SIDE OF THE SCALE WITH THE WEIGHTS. This provides the customer with a little extra merchandise, and in case the scale is somewhat in error in the storekeeper's favor, it will help to prevent the customer from being cheated.

HOWEVER, A SELLER WHO WEIGHED BOTH SIDES OF THE SCALE EVENLY MUST GIVE THE BUYER EXTRA GOODS: ONE IN TEN PARTS FOR LIQUIDS, ONE IN TWENTY PARTS FOR DRY PRODUCTS.

IN PLACES WHERE IT IS CUSTOMARY TO USE SMALL MEASURES, ONE MAY NOT USE LARGE ONES; WHERE IT IS CUSTOMARY TO USE LARGE MEASURES, ONE MAY NOT USE SMALL ONES.

IN PLACES WHERE IT IS CUSTOMARY TO LEVEL THE MEASURE, ONE MAY NOT HEAP IT; WHERE IT IS CUSTOMARY TO HEAP IT, ONE MAY NOT LEVEL IT. There is less likelihood of an honest mistake taking place or of intentional cheating going unnoticed if local custom is followed by all of the merchants in any given town.

Bava Batra 89b

תָּנוּ רַבָּנָן: אֵין עוֹשִׂין מִשְׁקָלוֹת לֹא שֶׁל בַּעַץ וְלֹא שֶׁל אֲבָר, וְלֹא שֶׁל גִּיסְטְרוֹן וְלֹא שֶׁל שְׁאָר מִינֵי מַתָּכוֹת, אֲבָל עוֹשֶׂה הוּא שֶׁל צוּנְמָא וְשֶׁל זְכוּכִית.

תָּנוּ רַבָּנָן: אֵין עוֹשִׂין הַמַּחַק שֶׁל דְּלַעַת — מִפְּנֵי שֶׁהוּא קַל, וְלֹא שֶׁל מַתֶּכֶת — מִפְּנֵי שֶׁהוּא מַכְבִּיד, אֲבָל עוֹשֵׂהוּ שֶׁל זַיִת וְשֶׁל אֱגוֹז, שֶׁל שִׁקְמָה וְשֶׁל אֶשְׁבְּרוֹעַ.

תָּנוּ רַבָּנָן: אֵין עוֹשִׂין אֶת הַמַּחַק צִדּוֹ אֶחָד עָב וְצִדּוֹ אֶחָד קָצַר.

לֹא יִמְחוֹק בְּבַת אַחַת, שֶׁהַמּוֹחֵק בְּבַת אַחַת — רַע לַמּוֹכֵר וְיָפֶה לַלּוֹקֵחַ, וְלֹא יִמְחוֹק מְעַט מְעַט — שֶׁרַע לַלּוֹקֵחַ וְיָפֶה לַמּוֹכֵר.

עַל כּוּלָּן אָמַר רַבָּן יוֹחָנָן בֶּן זַכַּאי: אוֹי לִי אִם אוֹמַר, אוֹי לִי אִם לֹא אוֹמַר; אִם אוֹמַר — שֶׁמָּא יִלְמְדוּ הָרַמָּאִין, וְאִם לֹא אוֹמַר — שֶׁמָּא יֹאמְרוּ הָרַמָּאִין: אֵין תַּלְמִידֵי חֲכָמִים בְּקִיאִין בְּמַעֲשֵׂה יָדֵינוּ.

אִיבַּעְיָא לְהוּ: אֲמָרָהּ אוֹ לֹא אֲמָרָהּ? "אָמַר רַב שְׁמוּאֵל בַּר רַב יִצְחָק: אֲמָרָהּ, וּמֵהַאי קְרָא אֲמָרָהּ: "כִּי יְשָׁרִים דַּרְכֵי ה' וְצַדִּקִים יֵלְכוּ בָם וּפֹשְׁעִים יִכָּשְׁלוּ בָם".

Gemara: **Our Rabbis taught in a** *baraita:* ONE MAY NOT MAKE WEIGHTS OF TIN, NOR OF LEAD, NOR OF AN ALLOY, NOR OF OTHER KINDS OF METAL, which are likely to corrode, BUT ONE SHOULD MAKE THEM OF STONE OR OF GLASS.

Our Rabbis taught in a *baraita:* ONE SHOULD NOT MAKE THE LEVEL OUT OF A GOURD, BECAUSE IT IS TOO LIGHT to properly level the produce, and the buyer may receive too much, NOR SHOULD ONE MAKE IT OUT OF METAL, BECAUSE IT IS TOO HEAVY; it may penetrate into the produce and not allow the buyer to receive what is due. BUT ONE SHOULD MAKE IT OF OLIVE WOOD, NUT, SYCAMORE, OR BOXWOOD.

Our Rabbis taught in a *baraita:* ONE MAY NOT MAKE THE LEVEL THICK ON ONE SIDE AND THIN ON THE OTHER lest a merchant use one side of the level for buying and the other for selling.

ONE MAY NOT LEVEL WITH ONE QUICK MOVEMENT, which could result in the produce not being fully leveled, FOR LEVELING IN THIS WAY IS BAD FOR THE SELLER AND GOOD FOR THE BUYER, AND ONE MAY NOT LEVEL BIT BY BIT, possibly penetrating the produce, FOR THIS IS BAD FOR THE BUYER AND GOOD FOR THE SELLER.

REGARDING ALL THESE DEVIOUS PRACTICES, RABBAN YOCHANAN BEN ZAKKAI SAID: WOE IS ME IF I SPEAK OF THESE PRACTICES, AND WOE

Rabban Yochanan ben Zakkai opposed the war against Rome (66–70 C.E.) and favored making an accommodation with the Roman authorities. He was the leading Sage in the period following the destruction of the Temple. He established an academy at Yavneh after the fall of the Temple and brought the Sages together there to reconstitute Jewish life. He introduced a number of ordinances to allow Jewish life to continue without a Temple and began, with his colleagues, to lay the foundations of Jewish law, which a century later became the Mishnah.

IS ME IF I DO NOT. IF I SPEAK OF THEM, THE CHEATERS MIGHT LEARN FROM MY WORDS, AND IF I DO NOT SPEAK OF THEM, THE CHEATERS MIGHT SAY, "THE SAGES ARE NOT ACQUAINTED WITH OUR PRACTICES."

Rav Samuel bar Rav Isaac was a third-century Babylonian Sage who immigrated to Palestine.

The Gemara then inquires as to the outcome of Rabban Yochanan ben Zakkai's dilemma: **The question was raised: Did he speak of these practices or not? Rav Samuel bar Rav Isaac said: He spoke of them and based his decision on the verse, "For the ways of *Adonai* are right. The righteous will follow them, but the wicked will stumble in them"** (Hos. 14:10). Rabban Yochanan ben Zakkai recognized that there were those who would misuse his teachings, but he believed that it was his duty to explain the law in order to guide those who wished to follow God's path.

What's Your Opinion?

Do you think that there should be laws mandating how often scales in stores and gas pumps at service stations need to be checked? In your opinion, did the Rabbis go too far in detailing the laws about measuring and weighing? Do you agree with the decision of Rabban Yochanan ben Zakkai to carefully explain what business practices are forbidden, despite the possibility that cheaters might learn from them?

Consider This Case

A recent article in the *New York Times* explained how certain businesses use bank accounts on offshore islands to avoid paying federal income taxes. The article gave details of what these businesses were doing and suggested that though it was legal, it was wrong. It indicated that Congress was considering legislation to prevent such activity.

Some people have criticized the *Times* for including in its article details of how taxes are avoided for fear that other businesses will learn from these practices and copy them. Others have said that it was necessary to include the details in the story to show how easy it is to avoid taxes, for this would encourage Congress to take action to prohibit it. What is your view on the matter?

Bava Batra 88a–b

Mishnah: **WHOLESALERS MUST CLEAN THEIR MEASURES ONCE IN THIRTY DAYS AND HOUSEHOLDERS ONCE EVERY TWELVE MONTHS.**

RABBAN SIMEON BEN GAMALIEL SAID: THIS STATEMENT SHOULD BE REVERSED.

STOREKEEPERS MUST CLEAN THEIR MEASURES TWICE A WEEK, WIPE THEIR WEIGHTS ONCE A WEEK, AND WIPE THEIR SCALES FOR EVERY SINGLE WEIGHING.

RABBAN SIMEON BEN GAMALIEL SAID: WHEN DO THESE RULES APPLY? WHEN LIQUIDS ARE SOLD, BUT FOR DRY PRODUCTS, IT IS NOT NECESSARY.

A STOREKEEPER MUST ALLOW THE SIDE OF THE SCALE WITH THE GOODS TO SINK A HANDBREADTH LOWER THAN THE SIDE OF THE SCALE WITH THE WEIGHTS.

HOWEVER, A SELLER WHO WEIGHED BOTH SIDES OF THE SCALE EVENLY MUST GIVE THE BUYER EXTRA GOODS: ONE IN TEN PARTS FOR LIQUIDS, ONE IN TWENTY PARTS FOR DRY PRODUCTS.

IN PLACES WHERE IT IS CUSTOMARY TO USE SMALL MEASURES, ONE MAY NOT USE LARGE ONES; WHERE IT IS CUSTOMARY TO USE LARGE MEASURES, ONE MAY NOT USE SMALL ONES.

IN PLACES WHERE IT IS CUSTOMARY TO LEVEL THE MEASURE, ONE MAY NOT HEAP IT; WHERE IT IS CUSTOMARY TO HEAP IT, ONE MAY NOT LEVEL IT.

Bava Batra 89b

Gemara: **Our Rabbis taught in a *baraita*: ONE MAY NOT MAKE WEIGHTS OF TIN, NOR OF LEAD, NOR OF AN ALLOY, NOR OF OTHER KINDS OF METAL, BUT ONE SHOULD MAKE THEM OF STONE OR OF GLASS.**

Our Rabbis taught in a *baraita*: ONE SHOULD NOT MAKE THE LEVEL OUT OF A GOURD, BECAUSE IT IS TOO LIGHT, NOR SHOULD ONE MAKE IT OUT OF METAL, BECAUSE IT IS TOO HEAVY; BUT ONE SHOULD MAKE IT OF OLIVE WOOD, NUT, SYCAMORE, OR BOXWOOD.

Our Rabbis taught in a *baraita:* ONE MAY NOT MAKE THE LEVEL THICK ON ONE SIDE AND THIN ON THE OTHER.

ONE MAY NOT LEVEL WITH ONE QUICK MOVEMENT, FOR LEVELING IN THIS WAY IS BAD FOR THE SELLER AND GOOD FOR THE BUYER, AND ONE MAY NOT LEVEL BIT BY BIT, FOR THIS IS BAD FOR THE BUYER AND GOOD FOR THE SELLER.

REGARDING ALL THESE DEVIOUS PRACTICES, RABBAN YOCHANAN BEN ZAKKAI SAID: WOE IS ME IF I SPEAK OF THESE PRACTICES, AND WOE IS ME IF I DO NOT. IF I SPEAK OF THEM, THE CHEATERS MIGHT LEARN FROM MY WORDS, AND IF I DO NOT SPEAK OF THEM, THE CHEATERS MIGHT SAY, "THE SAGES ARE NOT ACQUAINTED WITH OUR PRACTICES."

The question was raised: Did he speak of these practices or not? Rav Samuel bar Rav Isaac said: He spoke of them and based his decision on the verse, "For the ways of *Adonai* **are right. The righteous will follow them, but the wicked will stumble in them."**

Chapter Nine

Wrongdoing with Words

Bava Metzia 58b

כְּשֵׁם שֶׁאוֹנָאָה בְּמִקָּח וּמִמְכָּר כָּךְ אוֹנָאָה בִּדְבָרִים.

לֹא יֹאמַר לוֹ "בְּכַמָּה חֵפֶץ זֶה" וְהוּא אֵינוּ רוֹצֶה לִיקַּח.

אִם הָיָה בַּעַל תְּשׁוּבָה לֹא יֹאמַר לוֹ "זְכוֹר מַעֲשֶׂיךָ הָרִאשׁוֹנִים".

אִם הוּא בֶּן גֵּרִים לֹא יֹאמַר לוֹ "זְכוֹר מַעֲשֵׂה אֲבוֹתֶיךָ", שֶׁנֶּאֱמַר "וְגֵר לֹא תוֹנֶה וְלֹא תִלְחָצֶנּוּ".

תָּנוּ רַבָּנָן: "לֹא תוֹנוּ אִישׁ אֶת עֲמִיתוֹ" — בְּאוֹנָאַת דְּבָרִים הַכָּתוּב מְדַבֵּר.

אַתָּה אוֹמֵר בְּאוֹנָאַת דְּבָרִים, אוֹ אֵינוֹ אֶלָּא בְּאוֹנָאַת מָמוֹן?

כְּשֶׁהוּא אוֹמֵר "וְכִי תִמְכְּרוּ מִמְכָּר לַעֲמִיתֶךָ אוֹ קָנֹה מִיַּד עֲמִיתֶךָ" — הֲרֵי אוֹנָאַת מָמוֹן אָמוּר.

הָא מָה אֲנִי מְקַיֵּים "לֹא תוֹנוּ אִישׁ אֶת עֲמִיתוֹ"? בְּאוֹנָאַת דְּבָרִים.

הָא כֵּיצַד?

אִם הָיָה בַּעַל תְּשׁוּבָה אַל יֹאמַר לוֹ "זְכוֹר מַעֲשֶׂיךָ הָרִאשׁוֹנִים".

אִם הָיָה בֶּן גֵּרִים אַל יֹאמַר לוֹ "זְכוֹר מַעֲשֵׂה אֲבוֹתֶיךָ", אִם הָיָה גֵּר וּבָא לִלְמוֹד תּוֹרָה אַל יֹאמַר לוֹ "פֶּה שֶׁאָכַל נְבֵילוֹת וּטְרֵיפוֹת, שְׁקָצִים וּרְמָשִׂים בָּא לִלְמוֹד תּוֹרָה שֶׁנֶּאֶמְרָה מִפִּי הַגְּבוּרָה".

אִם הָיוּ יִסּוּרִין בָּאִין עָלָיו, אִם הָיוּ חֳלָאִים בָּאִין עָלָיו, אוֹ שֶׁהָיָה מְקַבֵּר אֶת בָּנָיו, אַל יֹאמַר לוֹ כְּדֶרֶךְ שֶׁאָמְרוּ לוֹ חֲבֵירָיו לְאִיּוֹב "הֲלֹא יִרְאָתְךָ כִּסְלָתֶךָ תִּקְוָתְךָ וְתֹם דְּרָכֶיךָ זְכָר נָא מִי הוּא נָקִי אָבָד".

אִם הָיוּ חַמָּרִים מְבַקְשִׁין תְּבוּאָה מִמֶּנּוּ, לֹא יֹאמַר לָהֶם "לְכוּ אֵצֶל פְּלוֹנִי שֶׁהוּא מוֹכֵר תְּבוּאָה" — וְיוֹדֵעַ בּוֹ שֶׁלֹּא מָכַר מֵעוֹלָם.

רַבִּי יְהוּדָה אוֹמֵר: "אַף לֹא יִתְלֶה עֵינָיו עַל הַמֶּקַח בְּשָׁעָה שֶׁאֵין לוֹ דָמִים, שֶׁהֲרֵי הַדָּבָר מָסוּר לַלֵּב, וְכָל דָּבָר הַמָּסוּר לַלֵּב נֶאֱמַר בּוֹ "וְיָרֵאתָ מֵאֱלֹהֶיךָ".

אָמַר רַבִּי יוֹחָנָן מִשּׁוּם רַבִּי שִׁמְעוֹן בֶּן יוֹחַאי: גָּדוֹל אוֹנָאַת דְּבָרִים מֵאוֹנָאַת מָמוֹן, שֶׁזֶּה נֶאֱמַר בּוֹ "וְיָרֵאתָ מֵאֱלֹהֶיךָ" וְזֶה לֹא נֶאֱמַר בּוֹ "וְיָרֵאתָ מֵאֱלֹהֶיךָ".

וְרַבִּי אֶלְעָזָר אוֹמֵר: זֶה בְּגוּפוֹ וְזֶה בְּמָמוֹנוֹ.

רַבִּי שְׁמוּאֵל בַּר נַחְמָנִי אָמַר: זֶה — נִתָּן לְהִישָּׁבוֹן, וְזֶה — לֹא נִתָּן לְהִישָּׁבוֹן.

תָּנֵי תַּנָּא קַמֵּיהּ דְּרַב נַחְמָן בַּר יִצְחָק: כָּל הַמַּלְבִּין פְּנֵי חֲבֵירוֹ בָּרַבִּים כְּאִילּוּ שׁוֹפֵךְ דָּמִים.

אָמַר לֵיהּ: שַׁפִּיר קָא אָמְרַתְּ, דְּחָזֵינָא לֵיהּ דְּאָזֵיל סוּמְקָא וְאָתֵי חִוְּרָא.

Mishnah: **JUST AS THERE IS WRONGDOING IN BUYING AND SELLING, SO THERE IS WRONGDOING WITH WORDS:**

ONE SHOULD NOT ASK A SELLER, "HOW MUCH DOES THIS ITEM COST?" IF ONE DOES NOT INTEND TO BUY IT.

The Mishnah departs from the matter of buying and selling to enlarge upon the subject of wrongdoing with words. **TO SOMEONE WHO IS A REPENTANT SINNER, ONE SHOULD NOT SAY, "REMEMBER YOUR PAST DEEDS."**

TO SOMEONE WHO IS A DESCENDANT OF CONVERTS, ONE SHOULD NOT SAY, "REMEMBER THE DEEDS OF YOUR ANCESTORS," FOR IT IS SAID, "YOU SHALL NOT WRONG OR OPPRESS A STRANGER" (Exod. 22:20).

The Gemara cites a *baraita,* which expands on the subject of wrongdoing with words: **Our Rabbis taught in a *baraita:* THE VERSE "YOU SHALL NOT WRONG ONE ANOTHER"** (Lev. 25:17) **SPEAKS OF VERBAL WRONGDOING.**

YOU SAY IT REFERS TO VERBAL WRONGDOING, BUT PERHAPS IT REFERS TO MONETARY WRONGDOING.

WHEN THE TORAH SAYS, "IF YOU SELL SOMETHING TO YOUR COMPANION OR BUY SOMETHING FROM YOUR COMPANION, YOU SHALL NOT WRONG ONE ANOTHER" (Lev. 25:14), **THAT VERSE REFERS TO MONETARY WRONGDOING.**

THEN HOW SHALL I EXPLAIN THE VERSE, "YOU SHALL NOT WRONG ONE ANOTHER?" (Lev. 25:17) **IT MUST REFER TO VERBAL WRONGDOING.**

The *baraita* reasons that each biblical verse has a distinct meaning. Thus if one verse refers to monetary wrongdoing, the other verse must refer to something else, in this case, verbal wrongdoing.

Having resolved the issue as to which biblical verse refers to monetary wrongdoing and which to verbal wrongdoing, the *baraita* turns to defining verbal wrongdoing: **WHAT THEN IS MEANT BY VERBAL WRONGDOING?**

TO SOMEONE WHO IS A REPENTANT SINNER, ONE SHOULD NOT SAY, "REMEMBER YOUR PAST DEEDS."

TO SOMEONE WHO IS A DESCENDANT OF CONVERTS, ONE SHOULD NOT SAY, "REMEMBER THE DEEDS OF YOUR ANCESTORS." TO SOMEONE WHO IS A CONVERT, AND WHO COMES TO STUDY TORAH, ONE SHOULD NOT SAY, "SHALL THE MOUTH THAT HAS EATEN FORBIDDEN FOODS COME TO STUDY TORAH, WHICH WAS SPOKEN BY THE MOUTH OF THE

ALMIGHTY?" Reminding sinners of their past deeds, or converts of their origins, is wrong because it is intended to embarrass and hurt.

IF AFFLICTIONS COME UPON SOMEONE, OR IF AN ILLNESS COMES UPON SOMEONE, OR TO SOMEONE WHO IS BURYING CHILDREN, ONE SHOULD NOT SPEAK THE WAY JOB'S FRIENDS SPOKE TO HIM, SAYING, "WHAT INNOCENT PERSON WAS EVER LOST?" (Job 4:7). Blaming people for being the cause of their own misfortune is another example of a terrible misuse of words.

TO ASS-DRIVERS WHO ARE SEEKING PRODUCE FROM SOMEONE, ONE SHOULD NOT SAY, "GO TO SO-AND-SO, WHO WILL SELL YOU PRODUCE," KNOWING THAT THAT PERSON DOESN'T SELL PRODUCE. This is an example of using words to intentionally mislead someone.

RABBI JUDAH SAID: ONE SHOULD NOT EVEN LOOK AT AN ITEM FOR SALE IF ONE DOES NOT HAVE THE MONEY WITH WHICH TO BUY IT. FOR EVEN THOUGH A PERSON'S THOUGHTS ARE GUARDED BY THE HEART, and other people may not be aware that one never had any intention of buying the item, it should not be done. AND CONCERNING ANY MATTER THAT IS GUARDED BY THE HEART, IT HAS BEEN SAID, "AND YOU SHALL FEAR YOUR GOD" (Lev. 25:17). A person's actions, including his use of words, should aim to heal, not to hurt, to lead, not to mislead. One should guard against wrongdoing or wrong speaking even when the wrong will never become known to others, for we all must face the judgement of our conscience and our God.

Rabbi Yochanan said in the name of Rabbi Simeon ben Yochai: Verbal wrongdoing is worse than monetary wrongdoing, for concerning verbal wrongdoing, it was said, "And you shall fear your God" (Lev. 25:17), but concerning monetary wrongdoing, it was not said, "And you shall fear your God" (Lev. 25:14).

And Rabbi Eleazar said: Verbal wrongdoing affects one's person, whereas monetary wrongdoing affects only one's money.

Rabbi Samuel bar Nachmani said: Monetary wrongdoing may be restored, whereas verbal wrongdoing cannot be restored.

Rabbi Eleazar ben Shammua is usually called Rabbi Eleazar, without his father's name, in the Talmud. He lived in the second century and was a prominent student of Rabbi Akiva.

Samuel bar Nachmani was a third-century Palestinian *Amora*. He was known for his expertise in *aggadah*.

A *Tanna* taught before Rabbi Nachman bar Isaac: WHEN SOMEONE SHAMES A COMPANION IN PUBLIC, IT IS LIKE SPILLING BLOOD.

Rabbi Nachman bar Isaac responded: You are right, for when someone is shamed in public, we see the face's redness depart while the whiteness enters.

What's Your Opinion?

Do you agree with the Mishnah that it is wrong to ask how much something costs if you have no intention of buying? Do you think that Rabbi Judah goes too far in saying that one should not even look at an item without having the money with which to buy it? Which is worse, cheating someone out of money or shaming someone in public?

Consider This Case

Before buying a large-screen TV, Joanne wanted to find out as much as she could about the various brands. First she went to TV City. She was helped there by a knowledgeable salesman who spent about forty-five minutes with her. She decided to buy a fifty-inch set. Then she went to Good Price and bought the TV there. The price was about $200 less at Good Price than it had been at TV City. Do you think that Joanne is guilty of wrongdoing with words for having taken forty-five minutes of the TV City salesman's time and then going to Good Price to purchase her TV?

REVIEWING THE TEXT

Bava Metzia 58b

Mishnah: **JUST AS THERE IS WRONGDOING IN BUYING AND SELLING, SO THERE IS WRONGDOING WITH WORDS:**

ONE SHOULD NOT ASK A SELLER, "HOW MUCH DOES THIS ITEM COST?" IF ONE DOES NOT INTEND TO BUY IT.

TO SOMEONE WHO IS A REPENTANT SINNER, ONE SHOULD NOT SAY, "REMEMBER YOUR PAST DEEDS."

TO SOMEONE WHO IS A DESCENDANT OF CONVERTS, ONE SHOULD NOT SAY, "REMEMBER THE DEEDS OF YOUR ANCESTORS," FOR IT IS SAID, "YOU SHALL NOT WRONG A STRANGER OR OPPRESS HIM."

Our Rabbis taught in a *baraita:* THE VERSE "YOU SHALL NOT WRONG ONE ANOTHER" SPEAKS OF VERBAL WRONGDOING.

YOU SAY IT REFERS TO VERBAL WRONGDOING, BUT PERHAPS IT REFERS TO MONETARY WRONGDOING.

WHEN THE TORAH SAYS, "IF YOU SELL SOMETHING TO YOUR COMPANION OR BUY SOMETHING FROM YOUR COMPANION, YOU SHALL NOT WRONG ONE ANOTHER." THAT VERSE REFERS TO MONETARY WRONGDOING.

THEN HOW SHALL I EXPLAIN THE VERSE, "YOU SHALL NOT WRONG ONE ANOTHER?" (LEV. 25:17) IT MUST REFER TO VERBAL WRONGDOING.

WHAT THEN IS MEANT BY VERBAL WRONGDOING?

TO SOMEONE WHO IS A REPENTANT SINNER, ONE SHOULD NOT SAY, "REMEMBER YOUR PAST DEEDS."

TO SOMEONE WHO IS A DESCENDANT OF CONVERTS, ONE SHOULD NOT SAY, "REMEMBER THE DEEDS OF YOUR ANCESTORS." TO SOMEONE WHO IS A CONVERT, AND WHO COMES TO STUDY TORAH, ONE SHOULD NOT SAY, "SHALL THE MOUTH THAT HAS EATEN FORBIDDEN FOODS COME TO STUDY TORAH, WHICH WAS SPOKEN BY THE MOUTH OF THE ALMIGHTY?"

IF AFFLICTIONS COME UPON SOMEONE, OR IF AN ILLNESS COMES UPON SOMEONE, OR TO SOMEONE WHO IS BURYING CHILDREN, ONE SHOULD NOT SPEAK THE WAY JOB'S FRIENDS SPOKE TO HIM, SAYING, "WHAT INNOCENT PERSON WAS EVER LOST?"

TO ASS-DRIVERS WHO ARE SEEKING PRODUCE FROM SOMEONE, ONE SHOULD NOT SAY, "GO TO SO-AND-SO, WHO WILL SELL YOU PRODUCE," KNOWING THAT THAT PERSON DOESN'T SELL PRODUCE.

RABBI JUDAH SAID: ONE SHOULD NOT EVEN LOOK AT AN ITEM FOR SALE IF ONE DOES NOT HAVE THE MONEY WITH WHICH TO BUY IT. FOR EVEN THOUGH A PERSON'S THOUGHTS ARE GUARDED BY THE HEART, CONCERNING ANY MATTER THAT IS GUARDED BY THE HEART, IT HAS BEEN SAID, "AND YOU SHALL FEAR YOUR GOD."

Rabbi Yochanan said in the name of Rabbi Simeon ben Yochai: Verbal wrongdoing is worse than monetary wrongdoing, for concerning verbal wrongdoing, it was said, "And you shall fear your God," but concerning monetary wrongdoing, it was not said, "And you shall fear your God."

And Rabbi Eleazar said: Verbal wrongdoing affects one's person, whereas monetary wrongdoing affects only one's money.

Rabbi Samuel bar Nachmani said: Monetary wrongdoing may be restored, whereas verbal wrongdoing cannot be restored.

A *Tanna* taught before Rabbi Nachman bar Isaac: WHEN SOMEONE SHAMES A COMPANION IN PUBLIC, IT IS LIKE SPILLING BLOOD.

Rabbi Nachman bar Isaac responded: You are right, for when someone is shamed in public, we see the face's redness depart while the whiteness enters.

Chapter Ten

Wrapping It Up

The purpose of "Wrapping It Up" is to encourage a review of the material covered in this book. It is suggested that students complete the answers to "Wrapping It Up" outside of the classroom, bring their answers to the class, and discuss them in class as a review lesson.

The Purchase Agreement

1. Why did the Sages rule that a sale is not final until the buyer actually takes possession of the goods?

2. How does the Gemara differentiate between punishment by God for breaking one's word and "the spirit of the Sages is not pleased with someone who backs out of a verbal commitment"?

3. According to the Gemara, if someone makes a down payment for a purchase, is the seller obliged to deliver goods equal to the amount of the down payment, or all of the promised goods?

What Is Included in a Sale?

The Mishnah teaches: If someone sold a wagon, it cannot be assumed that the mules were sold along with it. If someone sold some mules, it cannot be assumed that the wagon was sold along with them.

1. Why does Rabbi Judah dispute this ruling?

2. Under what circumstances does Rabbi Abahu make an exception to this ruling?

Product Liability

If someone sells an ox that is found to be a gorer, Rav says: This was an erroneous sale and the seller must refund the purchase price to the buyer, but Samuel says: The money does not have to be refunded because the seller can say to the buyer: I sold it to you for slaughtering.

1. There should be no dispute between Rav and Samuel. Simply find out whether the buyer usually buys for slaughtering or for plowing. But there is a dispute between Rav and Samuel because this is a case

   _____.

2. There should be no dispute. Simply see what the purchase price was. But there is a dispute because this is a case

   _____.

3. There should be no dispute because the buyer will get the same price for slaughtering and selling the ox as would be refunded upon returning it to the seller. But there is a dispute because _____.

4. There should be no dispute because the seller may not have the money to make a refund; it would be easier for the buyer just to slaughter and sell the ox and be sure of getting the money. There is a dispute because in this case

   _____.

5. In such a case, Rav rules that the sale is cancelled and the seller must refund the purchase price because _____, and Samuel rules that this principle stated by Rav applies in ritual matters but does not apply in monetary matters.

Allowing for Imperfection

1. The Mishnah allows one-twenty-fourth of a grain purchase to be bad grain. When would Rav Huna disallow this one-twenty-fourth?

2. The Mishnah rules that if two people deposit money with someone, one of them depositing 100 *zuz* and the other 200 *zuz*, and when they come to claim their deposit, they each claim the 200 *zuz*, the guardian should give each one 100 *zuz*, and the rest should remain with the guardian until Elijah comes. Why does Rabbi Yose dispute the ruling of the Mishnah?

3. Lending on interest is forbidden in biblical and in rabbinic law. What is the dispute between Rabbi Meir and the Rabbis regarding a promissory note that includes a provision for the payment of interest?

Overcharging and Underpaying

1. The Talmud considers an overcharge to be _____.

2. Buyers who think that they have been overcharged must return the goods for a refund within _____.

3. The Mishnah says that the law against cheating applies to a merchant who is underpaid just as it applies to a customer who is overcharged. But Rabbi Judah says that the law against cheating does not apply to a merchant who is underpaid.

   a) According to Rav Ashi, what does Rabbi Judah mean?

   b) According to Rav Nachman, what does Rabbi Judah mean?

Fraud

1. What is the purpose of the following restrictions?

   a) One may not mix produce from different sources.

   b) One may not sift just at the opening of the bin.

   c) One may not paint a person or an animal or utensils.

2. What is the reason for allowing the following practices?

   a) Strong wine may be mixed with weak wine.

   b) A seller may sift crushed beans to remove the refuse.

   c) Fringes may be put on a coat.

Competition

1. Rabbi Judah said: A storekeeper may not distribute parched grain or nuts to children in order to encourage them to shop in that store, but the Sages permit it because

   _____.

2. Furthermore, Rabbi Judah said: A storekeeper may not sell goods at less than the market price, but the Sages say:

   _____.

3. Rav Huna said: If the resident of an alley has set up a mill, and then another resident of the alley wants to set one up next door, the law is that the first one may prevent it, by making the claim, "You are obstructing my livelihood." What tannaitic source supports the view of Rav Huna?

4. Rav Huna the son of Rav Joshua disputed Rav Huna and said: The resident of an alley is not able to prevent another resident of the same alley from setting up a competing business. What tannaitic source supports the view of Rav Huna the son of Rav Joshua?

Scales and Measures

1. Wholesalers must clean their measures _____.

2. Householders must clean their measures _____.

3. Storekeepers must clean their measures _____.

4. Storekeepers must wipe their weights _____.

5. Storekeepers must wipe their scales _____.

Wrongdoing with Words

1. One should not ask a seller, "How much does this item cost?" if _____.

2. To someone who is a repentant sinner, one should not say, _____.

3. Rabbi Yochanan said in the name of Rabbi Simeon ben Yochai: Verbal wrongdoing is worse than monetary wrongdoing, for concerning verbal wrongdoing, it was said, "And you shall fear your God," but concerning monetary wrongdoing _____.

4. And Rabbi Eleazar said: Verbal wrongdoing affects one's person, whereas monetary wrongdoing _____.

5. Rabbi Samuel bar Nachmani said: Monetary wrongdoing may be restored, whereas verbal wrongdoing _____.

The Rabbis

1. Who was the disputant

   a) Of Hillel?

   b) Of Rav?

   c) Of Rava?

2. Place the following *Tannaim* in chronological order, beginning with Hillel:

   Hillel, Rabbi Meir, Rabban Yochanan ben Zakkai, Rabbi Judah HaNasi, Rabbi Akiva

3. Place the following *Amoraim* in chronological order, beginning with Rav:

   Rav, Rav Ashi, Rav Pappa, Rav Huna, Rava, Rav Nachman

Are the Laws Fair?

1. Do you find the Talmud's laws of buying and selling to be fair? Comment on each area of the law.

   a) Sticking to promises.

   b) Delivering quality products.

   c) Charging fair prices.

   d) Competition.

2. In general, would you say that the laws of the Talmud are more fair, less fair, or just about as fair as the laws of the community in which you live?